WOUNDED CONTINENT

Partnering with the
African Church
to Save the Dying

WOUNDED CONTINENT

Partnering with the
African Church
to Save the Dying

Tom Griner

FHI Books

ISBN 0-9677508-3-0

LC# 2005900427

Published by Father's Heart International (FHI) Books

P.O. Box 846

Bishop, CA 93515

1-800-873-1753

Printed in the United States of America

For more information, visit our website:

www.fhafrica.org

To Eric and Peggy Stovesand, friends, who for over thirty years have always been ready with a word of encouragement or a listening ear.

Acknowledgment

*L*ike a river that emerges from multiple streams, books come forth from various contributors. No one writes and publishes a book alone.

I am so very grateful to my wife Kathie, who first encouraged me to write the story of Father's Heart Africa. Also, Josef Rousek, Eric Stovesand and Steve Storey who whole-heartedly supported me in the process.

Many thanks to Nicole Nichols who worked to see the manuscript take a meaningful form and who did so in the light of prayerful considerations. I am grateful to Peggy Stovesand and David Sonner for their thoughtful suggestions and assistance in polishing the final work. John Schwartz is to be congratulated for his fine job in creating the cover design.

And then thanks to my three daughters, to Danielle for her encouragement to keep on writing, to Bethany for her helpful suggestions and to Lacy who spent hours preparing the manuscript for printing.

Thanks to you all.

TABLE OF CONENTS

CHAPTER 1 | HOPE FOR AFRICA

*O*ur entire team was on edge. It was June of 2004 and we had just crossed the border from the Democratic Republic of the Congo into Zambia, with less than 10 minutes to spare. The customs office closed at 6:00 P.M. and anyone with unfinished business with the custom agents would have to spend the night—no exceptions.

Even if we did get stranded overnight in *no man's land* (the land between the two borders) at the customs office, it would have been O.K. Less than two hours earlier, coming from holding a four day crusade (a series of outdoor evangelistic meetings) in Lubumbashi, we had been held up on the side of the road by five men who claimed to be police officers. They had stopped their four-door sedan in the middle of the highway, blocked our passage and signaled for us to pull over.

I hollered for our missionary driver Mike, to put the car in reverse and get our team—seven Americans, and one Congolese—out of there. But having lived in Africa for almost three years, he knew that to run in this situation was a sure invitation to escalated danger. So we reluctantly pulled over.

Our hearts raced as we watched the men hurry to our van, with automatic pistols tucked into their jeans.

"Why have you stopped us?" we asked.

Their excuse was that they had seen one of our team members videotaping the countryside, and they claimed that it was illegal to do so. The men were not dressed in police uniforms and it was obvious that they had been drinking. So we listened up.

In French the leader said, "You must come with us. One of my men will ride with you. Follow us." All I could think about was an article I had read a month prior about how most of the killing and robbery that happens in Africa, occurs in desolate places like we were in at that moment!

As our driver courteously argued with the men, I wondered how I might get out of the van if things turned ugly. I was in the very back. My mind raced trying to think of the quickest exit.

After nearly thirty-five minutes of intense wrangling, the roving tax collectors agreed to let us pass if we paid them a fine of $300. I was relieved. We paid the money and left hurriedly, each of us only imagining what could have happened. Rose, the young woman who had been doing the videotaping, sat crying. Someone else said, "Praise the Lord." I was mortified. So, you understand what I mean when I say, I was glad just to be stuck in *no man's land*, (though it is itself a dangerous and crime-infested place). Needless to say, it was absolutely pure joy when we saw Pastor Somwe come out of the customs office smiling with our passports in hand. Until you have tried to pass one of these African borders, you can't really understand the relief I felt at that moment.

A native Congolese, Pastor Somwe had been nothing but a blessing since the moment we met him. Being from the Congo, he spoke French and Swahili. He also pastored a church in Zambia, meaning he was fluent in a couple of its local languages, as well as English. When you're in Africa there's nothing like having someone who not only speaks the language, but knows the ropes as well. That was Pastor Somwe.

As the border gates swung open and our Toyota van passed safely into Zambia, I didn't even look back. I just breathed a sigh of relief. We all breathed a sigh of relief.

A Scourge Beyond What We Can Imagine

Born and raised in the United States, I am in no way an expert on Africa. However, I have been there enough to realize that the people are strong, but wounded. They are strong in work, resilient and resourceful in life, and patient in adversity. But they are wounded and battered by the continual gale force winds of poverty, disease, and conflict.

Poverty and disease haunt the African people. More than half of the population live on less than $1 per day. While economic growth is lifting millions out of poverty in other parts of the developing world, Africa's economy is barely keeping up with its expanding population and its growing problems. Of all the nations of the world, Africa is the only continent to have become poorer in the last 25 years.

Death and disease, especially the HIV/AIDS plague, have devastated young and old. Life expectancy is lower in sub-Saharan Africa than in any other continent in the world. In Zambia the life expectancy at birth has plummeted to 32 years. It is estimated that nearly 1.2 million people in Zambia alone are infected with the HIV/AIDS virus.[1] It is a scourge beyond imagining.

I have stood on the fresh mounds of dirt at the Chunga cemetery (in Lusaka, Zambia), looking out as far as I could see over endless graves and ones yet to receive their dead. These graves had no markers other than a stick or little wooden cross beside some wind shredded plastic floral arrangement. Almost everyday, a small army of grave- diggers (as many as 100) is busily burying as many as 50 bodies, and they are running out of space.

As HIV/AIDS blazes through the countryside, killing the farmers, teachers, mothers and fathers of the nation, millions of children are left orphaned in the ashes. In Zambia alone it is estimated that there are a million orphan children.[2] Many of who, rejected and abandoned with nowhere to go, live on the streets and sleep in the gutters. With no one to care for them, feed them or provide the fees of public school, they go hungry and uneducated. They spend their days and nights scratching out a living by begging, stealing, or selling themselves as prostitutes. To compound the tragedy, it is upon the weary shoulders of such children that the future of these African nations rests.

But there is more than the flame of disease that has crippled the African continent. Any perusal of its turbulent history quickly reveals that in most nations the blood has flowed, and to say that there have been human rights violations would be an understatement. Only Africans themselves know how deeply they have suffered. But there is hope.

A new day is dawning in sub-Saharan Africa, as God raises up a new generation of pastors, evangelists and Christian workers. These national Christians are gripped with the realities their people face and are filled with an urgent compassion to do everything possible to see their countrymen come to the salvation found only in Jesus Christ. One such pastor is J. Mumba.

A Ray of Hope

If there is anything that binds most people in rural Zambia, traditional beliefs rank top on the list. National pastors must seek God's face and be filled with the Spirit of God if they are to effectively come against the spiritual powers that bind so many in Africa. Pastor J. Mumba meets everyday with fellow Christians to seek God for a breakthrough in the town of Chipata (in the Eastern providence of Zambia). Here the people are strongly bound to their traditional beliefs, particularly that of *vinamwali*, a ceremonial initiation of girls who reach puberty, and *ngoma*, African songs, chants and dances performed with drums as a means of spiritual and social healing.

Pastor J. Mumba and others, unwavering in their preaching of the gospel, go door to door urging the people to turn from their sins to true life in Jesus Christ.

By God's grace, their work is bearing fruit. Many people have come to the knowledge that Jesus is the only way, truth and life.

"Once, we prayed for a woman who was blind, and we saw God heal her," said Pastor J. Mumba. Miracles like these make the case for Christ even stronger in the eyes of those who know the reality of spiritual powers.

"Through prayer and faith in God, we have seen people once bound by traditions set free, (even local wizards and witches). At most of the evangelistic crusades we have held, people brought their witchcraft charms for us to destroy in the fire.

"We even saw many village chiefs surrender to Christ. This is tremendous! There was one chief who had three jars containing different charms that were passed on to him and which he believed had great powers to protect him. He listened to us preach that Jesus Christ is the true God and powerful over all. Through our witness, he gave his life to Christ. He also surrendered his jars of charms and told us to destroy them."

"As we started to disciple and teach him Bible lessons, he saw areas in his life that needed to change. It was moving to see him embrace the truth that Jesus is God."

"Unfortunately, he passed away shortly after turning to the Lord.

But we praise God, knowing that he was rescued from hell before it was too late. Today, he is with Jesus."

This scenario is being repeated all throughout Africa as national pastors and evangelists give their lives to preach the gospel. In the midst of great political, social and physical turmoil they labor to bring the only true hope to their countrymen—the gospel of Jesus Christ.

As part of the Body of Christ, God is offering us the privilege of playing a vital role in what He is doing among the nations of the earth. This is the story of how I responded to that invitation, and the blessing and lessons that have come from it. It has been a remarkable journey. God is offering you the privilege of having a part to play as well.

At Chunga cemetery in Lusaka, Zambia--graves as far as the eye can see.

Chunga cemetery receives another victim courtesy of the *ugly sisters*--Hunger and AIDS.

PART I | PREPARING THE GROUND

Prayers offered
to the wooden
idol San Simón.

The cobble streets of Zunil, Guatemala
where the wooden idol San Simón resides.

Chapter 2 | Wooden Idols

*A*nother rock landed with a thud on the tin awning protecting us from the nightly drizzle. This was our third night of preaching in the small village of Zunil, Guatemala. Some of the Quiche Indians were obviously not happy with us being in their close-knit community. About 300 had gathered to hear us that night. Many stood in the background with their arms crossed and blank expressions on their faces.

I preached with two interpreters, one translating into the Quiche language and the other translating into Spanish. During the intervals, between my preaching and the interpretations, I thought about the rocks hitting the roof and the stoic stares of the men that attended our meeting. I wondered if my preaching was making any difference. Then, in the midst of my musings, came what I knew to be a word from the Lord: "*I have called you to do this. Preach this gospel and don't be afraid.*"

Those words seemed to hang in mid-air as I collected myself to deliver the next thought of my sermon. At that moment, a sense of confidence and destiny filled my soul. Despite the seeming hardness of hearts and the looks of rebuff, I took courage and continued to preach.

My Heart Burned within Me

I had come to Guatemala with Kathie, my wife of just three months, and her brother Paul. Our purpose was to attend language school and to conduct evangelistic crusades.

The vision that led me to Guatemala had been placed in my heart a couple of years earlier while attending a theology school in Anaheim, California. During my third year of school, a man came to talk about his life as an evangelist. The man was T. L. Osborn, a crusade evangelist who for more than 30 years had traveled the world with his wife, Daisy, preaching to the masses and praying for the sick.

He was not a high-powered preacher, but told simple stories of his experiences with the power of God. He told of multitudes being saved, the blind seeing, deaf hearing, cripples walking and churches being planted. I had read about those types of things happening in the book of Acts, but never before had I met a man actually doing them today.

As T. L. Osborn continued to speak, it was as though I awoke from a dream. I was so deeply moved by his words. With each word I listened to, it was as though I could feel something rising out of my soul, a fountain of desire saying, "*You can do that. You can preach the gospel. You can pray for the sick and win the world to Jesus.*" Like the disciples on the Emmaus road in Luke 24:32, my heart burned within me.

When I left that meeting, I was a different man. I had a new zeal to proclaim the gospel and see God perform signs and wonders, drawing people to His side in repentance. I was so compelled that the next day I went out on the streets searching for someone to preach to. There, on the corner of Harbor Boulevard and Grand Avenue in Anaheim, California, I preached publicly for the first time—to the people as they sat in their cars stopped at the traffic light.

A few weeks later, I planned a series of evangelistic meetings at the Santa Ana High School auditorium in Santa Ana, California. Excited, my friends and I distributed more than 8,000 flyers door to door. We also advertised the event on radio and television. The week of the meetings finally came, and though less than 100 attended each night, I was thrilled to preach. These were small beginnings, but beginnings nonetheless. I had been set ablaze with a vision for world evangelism and now I was launching out.

Unexpected Challenges

But now here I was in Guatemala, on my first foreign mission field experience. It was different than I expected and extremely more difficult than I could have imagined.

From the moment we landed in Guatemala City, our language deficiency transformed simple, everyday events into major challenges. None of us knew much Spanish other than *buenos díaz*—"good morning."

Obtaining a bus ticket and finding the right bus to our destination was like a nightmare.

While in Guatemala our plan was to live with a Guatemalan family in the countries second largest city, Quetzaltenango located about 120 miles west of Guatemala City. When we finally arrived at our home in Quetzaltenango the challenges didn't stop. Our new family, as precious as they were, had flea-infested dogs. As a result, we had man-eating fleas in our socks almost everyday and sometimes in our beds. And then, the difference found in the bacterial flora in the food wreaked havoc on my intestines. I lost 15 pounds from diarrhea in the first two weeks. Having very little money, we walked almost everywhere, always calculating the distance to the next *baño* (toilet).

Adding to our misery, we had a five-hour, one-on-one Spanish lesson each day. Though learning the language was one of the goals of our trip, our teachers, who didn't speak a word of English, were without mercy. They instructed us like Marine drill sergeants. It was absolutely grueling. Yet in the midst of many negative trials—diarrhea, flea bites, hurting heads and lack of funds—there was one positive thing: we had a lot of zeal for Jesus.

Encounter with the Idol

Each week our language teachers would take us into the community for cultural encounters. One such outing took us by bus to the small village of Zunil, located a few miles outside of Quetzaltenango.

The village of Zunil was a Mayan agricultural center nestled in the heart of the Sierra Madres, 8,000 feet above sea level. There were no churches other than a Catholic church and a bizarre cult that worshiped an idol called San Simón.

When we first saw this mannequin idol dressed as a cowboy with sunglasses, we were greatly disturbed. We wondered how people could be so darkened as to worship such a lifeless thing. We watched as people filed by bowing to San Simón, lighting candles and offering prayers to this god of wood. Its keepers would place a lit cigarette in its wooden mouth and pour whiskey down its wooden throat. It was an unbelievable sight:

One devotee who had come to speak with San Simón went through a ritual with a *brujo*, a prayer man. She had purchased a basket of offerings at the shack next to the holy room. It contained purple, blue, white and green small taper candles, cigars, cigarettes, 6 eggs, limes, hard red, white and green Christmas candy, kindling, incense, salt and two bottles of Quetzalteca, a Guatemalan brand of [strong liquor]. They were to be blessed by San Simón during her session with him. The prayer man brushed her body with branches of some kind of tree on which he had squeezed lime juice.

The woman knelt at the foot of San Simón, like a child at the lap of her father. She talked to San Simón while the prayer man chanted incantations. She stroked the idol's hands and leg, imploring something about her son . . . The *brujo* removed San Simón's hat and put it on her head. Then she stood and he put San Simón's arm around her. She began crying and pleading louder. He motioned for her to kneel and stand a few more times, charging the ritual with electricity that filled the room . . . The prayer man and his helper put a cigarette in a holder, placed it in the idol's mouth and lit it.

After a while, they took a bottle of Quetzalteca, which they had placed in San Simón's lap and, leaning the idol far back in his chair, poured the contents of the bottle down his throat. They also gave the woman a small vial of liquor from the bottle (later released into a large aluminum bowl beneath the throne and resold as sacred liquor).[3]

As we stood watching the devotees of San Simón, we felt smothered by the intense demonic presence that filled the room. Provoked by all I had seen and grieved in my heart, I determined something must be done. These people must know the truth. I must preach the gospel to the people of this dark city. Only later did we learn that the last missionaries attempting to preach in this village had been run out of town with stones.

CHAPTER 3 | BE CAREFUL WHAT YOU ASK FOR

*A*re you the man who wants to preach in Zunil?"
It was early in the afternoon as Kathie and I sipped a Coke in a café just days after our experience with San Simón. The stranger's question took us by surprise. Since our encounter with the idol, our hearts had been gripped over the darkness that the people of Zunil lived in. There was no way of forgetting it. Images of that wooden demon and the people giving it homage haunted us. We had earnestly sought the Lord in prayer, asking Him to open up the doors for us to preach the gospel there.

However great the burden was, we still had no idea how we were going to do it. We had talked with the family we stayed with and our language school director about our desire to hold a crusade in Zunil, but neither of them could offer any help.

We sat in the café discussing the seeming impossibility of it happening. We didn't know anyone, couldn't speak the language and knew of no translators. Neither did we have any sound equipment. It all seemed so hopeless. In frustration, I said to Kathie that there was no way this thing was going to happen. The obstacles were just too great. Disappointed, we resolved to put the whole idea out of our minds. My last comment was, "If the Lord wants me to preach, then He will have to give me a personal invitation and put the whole thing together." That's when the man appeared with his startling question.

In broken English he asked, "Are you the man who wants to preach in Zunil?" Amazed, I answered with a hesitant, "Yes. I am."

The man was Pastor José Menni, the superintendent of the Church of God for Western Guatemala. Hearing about our desire to preach in Zunil, he had come to give us a personal invitation. After some further introductions, Pastor Menni began to tell us that he knew a young pastor named Mariano who was seeking to plant a church in Zunil and could help us set up a crusade. Known to be a hard worker and one eager to win his country to Christ, Pastor Mariano already cared for a small church in a village near Zunil. Knowing how the people of Zunil were given over to idolatry and drunkenness, his heart yearned to minister there.

On hearing this, I could hardly contain myself. Pastor Menni said he would make arrangements for us to meet with Pastor Mariano the next day. When he said good-bye and departed, Kathie and I looked at each other in wonderment. I had my special invitation from the Lord. He was putting it all together.

The following day we met with Pastor Mariano who was as happy about the ministry opportunity as we were. He brought along a friend who could speak just enough English to help us begin planning. Though not without some challenges, all the logistics for the crusade came together, everything from the perfect location, to borrowed sound equipment and the necessary translators. The date was set. In two weeks time, we were going to preach in the village of the mannequin idol.

Kathie, Paul and I were elated and prayed like never before. This was our dream and now it was coming to pass! Everything had so miraculously transpired that we just knew these were going to be important meetings.

Difficult Ministry

When the time of the crusade arrived, it was drizzling and foggy. Still, some 300 indians gathered each night to hear us. With arms folded, their eyes were filled with reserve and suspicion. A thick cloud of oppression seemed to hang over us all. This was not what I had anticipated.

Each night I preached and each night I was met with blank stares. I could not help but wonder if any of this was making a difference. The meetings weren't exciting and miraculous like the stories I heard from T. L. Osborn. Instead, they were hard and almost depressing—like what I would imagine plowing a rocky field to be. I sought courage though, in what I knew the Lord had spoken to me: "*I have called you to do this. Preach this gospel and don't be afraid.*" That was my one refuge.

When the week of preaching was finally concluded, the drizzle stopped, the fog lifted and seven people had come to the Lord, three of which were children. It wasn't very impressive for an evangelist.

Returning to our rooms that night, Kathie and Paul were silent. Paul was particularly disappointed, though he didn't say so at the time. He had come with an expectation to see great things. We had all come with that expectation. I had boasted about what I knew God was going to do and shared the great stories I had heard from T. L. Osborn. Our experience so far was but a trickle in comparison. Still, I had the assurance that I was in the perfect will of God.

A few weeks later our time in language school came to an end. Saying our good-byes, we prepared to catch a bus to Guatemala City to connect with our flight back to the United States.

Before we boarded the bus, Pastor Mariano arrived to wish us farewell. Beaming, he gave me a little plaque inscribed with the date and place of the Zunil crusade and how many were saved. At the bottom was his engraved signature. I could see in his face that there were no failed expectations with him—only gratitude. We said our good-byes and boarded the bus.

While our bus lumbered its way up and out of the valley, I looked back on Quetzaltenango, our home for the last several weeks. I could see Zunil off in the distance, my mind reminiscing the difficult nights of preaching. Now everything was quickly slipping into the past. But the lessons learned would come again to teach me in future days.

A Man of Sacrifice

Our return to the United States was uneventful. The pace of life in Guatemala made the days at home in California seem dull in comparison.

Six months edged by until one day we received a letter from Pastor Mariano. I brought the letter to Kathie and we opened it together with anticipation. He wrote of how the crusade we held opened up an effectual door of ministry in Zunil. From this, he was able to successfully start two new churches in the village.

He concluded his letter with the sorrow of personal tragedy. One of his daughters had gotten sick and died. He didn't give many details, but it was obvious that he and his family were deeply sorrowed. Even so, he declared that the work of the gospel must continue. Everyday, Pastor Mariano continued to walk to Zunil to meet with, pray for, encourage and teach the people of the village.

To be honest, I don't know that I could have done what he did. He lived in scarcity, labored in a demonized community, suffered the loss of a child and still declared, "The work of the ministry must continue."

As we read this, our hearts broke. We thought, "What a sacrificial commitment this man has to the work of God." We felt stirred and knew we had to make a return trip to visit this pastor and the new churches.

Within the next few months we were able to make a trip back to Guatemala to visit the pastor. Upon seeing him, he immediately took us to visit one of the newly planted churches.

We reached Zunil about 7 P.M. and twisted our way down a narrow cobblestone road to a little wood and tin building. The sound of praise filled the air. More than 60 villagers (many dressed in their brightly colored traditional dress, and women with babies slung in blankets on their backs) had gathered to worship the Lord. How different the atmosphere was from our first experience in this village of the idol San Simón! We were filled with joy at what the Lord had done through this seemingly insignificant native pastor.

Looking at the beaming faces of these new believers, Kathie and I felt somewhat like parents ourselves. We remembered all that had happened during our first stay and how we left a bit disappointed thinking that our seven days of preaching resulted in such little fruit.

Now we saw just how narrow our view was of what God could do. What seemed to have been a failure as an evangelistic outreach, turned out to be the seeds of two new churches. The Lord reminded me never to despise small beginnings or to underestimate the power of the gospel.

A New Understanding

Having just graduated from seminary and this being my first attempt at a foreign crusade, Zunil seemed to be the beginning of my ministry. In reality, it turned out to be the beginning of a major shift in the way I thought, one that would pave the road of ministry ahead of me.

Like most young preachers eager to serve God, I went into this ministry opportunity seeing myself as the anointed preacher ready to win the world to Christ. I expected to waltz into those villages with the power of God and see the miraculous happen and return home with stories like the ones I had heard from T. L. Osborn.

But that wasn't the mind of the Lord.

In the years and experiences following that first crusade in Zunil, God began to graciously open my eyes to the truth of what He was doing, through a powerful tool I was only beginning to recognize.

But this didn't come to full light until Costa Rica, 1984.

Pastor Mariano preaching in the crusade in Zunil.

The newlyweds, Tom and Kathie Griner, just weeks before their first mission trip to Guatemala in 1980.

CHAPTER 4 | REALIZING THE PLAN OF GOD

*F*ollowing our missionary experiences in Guatemala, Kathie's and my life changed a great deal. For one thing we became immersed in starting new churches in Nevada and California. Along with that, we were also learning about being parents to our two baby girls, Danielle and Bethany.

Though we were thankful for the ministry opportunities the Lord gave us in the United States, we continued to yearn for the nations of the world. Finally, in the summer of 1984 it was all too much. In a bold decision we sold everything we owned—our car, all our furniture, everything, including baby cribs—and moved our family to Costa Rica to serve the Lord as missionaries. Though our family and some friends thought that maybe we were being a little hasty, we knew we could do nothing else.

Arriving in San José, the capitol of Costa Rica, our strategy was to once again study Spanish and preach crusades. And again, God's strategy was that and more.

With much effort, we got all our suitcases and boxes through customs and were met by a friend who took us to our new residence, a house that had belonged to some missionary friends who were on furlough.

We settled in and unpacked our things, and soon discovered that our new home was infested with fleas. Before I realized what was happening, my three-year-old daughter, Danielle, had more than three dozen bites covering her little body. I instantly went looking for some bug spray but was not able to find any. Finally, I called our one friend and he brought over some insecticide. After spraying the whole place down, the crisis subsided and we went to bed, drained.

The days and weeks ahead turned out to be much better than our first night in this new land. We had come to Costa Rica in a season of tremendous revival. There was a sovereign move of God taking place all over the country. People were being saved, new churches were springing up and almost everyone seemed hungry for the Lord. As a result, I received many invitations to preach and was able to travel around the country seeing first hand what the Lord was doing.

It Makes Me Sick

During these times of travel and preaching, one thing became clear . . . as much as the Costa Ricans appreciated the ministries from abroad, there were some underlying resentments.

I began to see this one day in a conversation with a local pastor I knew. In all sincerity he asked me, "Why do you people send missionaries here who have no anointing or spiritual authority?" Though somewhat taken back by his question, I asked him to explain.

Continuing, he told me stories about missionaries who came to preach in the churches of Costa Rica, who were more filled with attitudes of superiority and condescension than with the Holy Spirit. They often treated the national pastors as if they were invisible or just plan inept— little children needing to be instructed. Many had only one agenda, to establish their own particular denomination at all costs. And in the process they often had very little appreciation for what God had already been doing among the local pastors. The local ministry was nothing more than a stepping-stone for these missionaries with their supposed superior agendas and ability.

The pastor said, "In reality, they are making prostitutes out of us." I asked what he meant. "The pastors are in such need of resources that they will often receive almost anyone who might be able to help them with their ministry. They willingly overlook the parental attitudes that often pervade the foreign missionaries and suffer the price of condescension and control to find favor for resources. Then the visiting ministers go home with embellished stories of success when, in actuality, they were merely riding off of the anointing and achievement of the national ministry. The local pastors obtain the resources they so desperately need, and the visiting pastors get an ego boost." He then said, "It all makes me sick."

What he said shocked me.

Yet, it also caused me to think deeply as to the truth of his statement. He had exposed something and it was in me too.

Deliver Me from Ethnocentricity

I first went to the mission field eager to serve the Lord. I wanted to see His power made known, to see blind eyes opened, both spiritually and physically. Yet in the midst of all my zeal and desire to be used by God, my heart was extremely self-centered.

When it came to ministry, I was fairly self-focused. All I could think about was my role as the preacher—how I was going to make a difference in the nations, how I was going to pray for people and how I was going to see the sick healed. I was blind to most everything else.

I thought back on my first trip to Guatemala, remembering the national pastor who so willingly helped me hold my first crusade and who stayed long after I was gone, starting churches and making disciples of the new believers. He was the one who had the larger share of ministry responsibility. He was the real hero. But, just like the Costa Rican pastor said, I came home speaking of how great God worked—through *me*.

In my zeal as a novice, I had little understanding of what God desired to do on a larger scale, with myself not as the center, but a vital player willing to yield to His will and His ways.

My Costa Rican friend was not just a disgruntled pastor. He was saying something vitally important, something my North American ears needed to hear.

Anthropologists call it *ethnocentricity*—the tendency to view one's cultural values, beliefs and norms as superior to any other culture or society. Americans are notorious for this though we don't do it maliciously; we are just convinced that our way is always the best way, even when it comes to ministry. This was the problem my pastor friend was describing.

In essence, he was saying, "God is with *us*, too. We have His Spirit. We can preach this gospel and start new churches. We are able to lead."

The concerns he voiced were not one-sided either. Along with being upset at the way ministers from other countries treated national pastors, he was also concerned with the way the national pastors would so eagerly *pimp* the ministry for resources. He was tired of the tendencies toward exploitation that were occurring on both sides.

I now understand he was not only expressing the immaturity and selfishness of certain foreign ministers in their ethnocentristic views, but he was also expressing the tension of changing roles between the national churches and those who had *parented* them in the gospel. The national ministers were coming of age. They had received the gospel years earlier. Now they were growing up in Christ. They were thinking and acting like young adults, ready to go out on their own and make their own way. They were taking responsibility for the spread of the gospel in their homeland. And this was also the cause of tension with the foreign missionaries.

The role of the missionary needed to change: from *parent* to that of *partner*.

Native Soil

Edgar and Carlos Chacon are good examples of what I am talking about. Having grown up in Costa Rica, these brothers became successful businessmen. In the late 70's, they heard the gospel and soon their lives were involved in fruitful ministry.

Far from being products of North American denominationalism or colonialism, they were strictly homegrown. They were born in Costa Rica, saved in a Costa Rican church, taught by Costa Rican mentors and used their own resources to start a Costa Rican church. These new converts burned to share the Good News with their fellow countrymen, and it wasn't too long until they started a thriving church in San José that grew to several thousand members.

It was easy to see that the Chacon brothers didn't need someone from the United States or Great Britain to lead them by the hand. I quickly came to understand that these men had not just come of age, but they themselves were qualified *parents*—actively making true disciples, planting churches and sending out missionaries. I knew I could learn from them. How different from the typical idea that the North American missionary is the teacher and the poor national is always the learner-child.

These brothers were anointed leaders in their own right, men of passion and grace who could not only teach the Bible and equip the believers, but also administrate the ministry. They were men who knew God and could—*and did*—preach, pray and weep over their flocks. They were sharp and gifted men of God. Poor? Yes. Having a different method of doing things? Very often. But called and filled with the Spirit of God nonetheless. My understanding of missions began to be challenged. My American mentality was being changed.

The Changing Face of Missions

Like no other, the Chacon brothers were especially fitted to do the work of Christ in their own country. Across the world today, this is showing itself to be true: national Christians are leading the way in reaching their nations for Christ.

From Asia to Africa, the Lord is calling out a people who are ready to give their lives for the sake of seeing their countrymen come to the truth found only in Jesus Christ. Stories of martyrdom, previously only heard of in the history of Christian missions, are springing up like fresh shoots from the ground. The persecution that they, our brothers and sisters in Christ, face is grueling. Yet still they labor, giving their all—literally—for the sake of Christ.

Waves of such missionaries are being trained, mobilized and sent in unprecedented numbers. The face of Christian missions is changing. It is becoming the face of the third world Christian.

This evolving of Christian missions is reason for much rejoicing. Like a father who desires to see his son grow into all that he should be, so we Western believers should rejoice in the Body of Christ in third world nations that is coming of age. Having received the gospel in times past, these believers have now grown into men and women capable of doing the work of Christ in their own land and beyond.

Still, many of us in the Western world have not perceived this shift. Stuck in the attitude that we know best, we hesitate to let go of methods that have worked in the past, ultimately hindering the potential inroads national pastors could make within their own countries. If not for the lessons from Zunil and Costa Rica, along with the grace of God, I would also still be blind to the great privilege and new role the Lord is offering to His church in the West: coming alongside our brothers and sisters around the world as they labor for Christ in their own nations.

CHAPTER 5 | DREAMS OF AFRICA

*A*fter a year of language school and preaching in Costa Rica, Kathie and I returned to the States. Kathie was pregnant with our third child Lacy, and the due date was drawing near. I also thought it would be a good opportunity to shore up our sinking financial base.

It wasn't long though, before Kathie and I were again absorbed in living with our pursuit of foreign missions being temporally pushed to the *back burner* of our hearts. We found ourselves once again pastoring a church and busy in the swirl of raising now, three daughters all of whom were under the age of four—Kathie's memory of washing and ironing cloth diapers in Costa Rica now fading.

During this time, to try and answer my call to missions, I began to mobilize dozens of short-term mission outreaches to countries around the world like Russia, Central and South America, and the Caribbean. During these trips I taught seminars on how to minister in the gifts of the Spirit and conducted crusades. One of the benefits of these outings was the experience that the people who accompanied me gained. I always took time to teach and encourage them to minister thus helping them acquire valuable training in hands on ministry.

Yet, despite this successful outlet of ministry, I still found myself becoming increasingly restless in regards to missions. I knew there was something more the Lord wanted to do through me. My unrest drove me to seek the Lord for answers.

Visions of Africa

While praying one morning during this season, I sensed the Lord speaking to my heart: *"If you will go to the middle of the earth and put up your sails, I will fill them."*

The words went deep into my soul. I knew this was the Spirit of God. As I considered what the words meant, I thought of the equator and particularly Africa. I got out a map and studied it. While I looked, I felt as though Central Africa and beyond was the harvest field the Lord was calling me to.

Then I had two other words that I believed were from the Lord. This time they came as dreams.

The dreams came almost back-to-back, both including an encounter with the famous German evangelist, Reinhard Bonnke. I had never met the man, but had heard some of his sermons and read about his gospel crusades in Africa.

In the first dream, Reinhard called me on the telephone and asked me to be his disciple. He explained that he had called several men and was inviting all of us to join him in his work in Africa.

In the second dream, I was with Reinhard in Africa. He had two shovels. Handing one shovel to me, Reinhard instructed me to put it into the ground where he put his. We were standing next to a large ravine. As I put my shovel in alongside his, the whole side of the ravine caved in, but we remained standing.

From these two dreams, I knew the Lord was trying to speak to me. They were mounting confirmation for the direction of my future. I knew I was going to preach the gospel in Africa and many souls would be saved. Though, I didn't know exactly how, when or where, I was delighted by what God was going to do.

But I had never been to Africa. I knew no one in Africa. I had no idea how God was going to bring this about. I simply hid these words in my heart and trusted the Lord to carry out the work that He started.

Then I got a phone call.

Two years after the dreams, I received a call from a good friend, Ron Sutton. He was going to Zambia to teach a Bible conference and hold a gospel crusade. He was looking for a companion and asked me to go along with him.

Having just returned from a 14-day mission trip to Ecuador, I felt too pressed to be making another trip out of the country so soon. The church I was pastoring was very demanding. We also had a television ministry in which we produced and aired a program on a weekly basis. I was just too busy to be leaving again.

I told Kathie my decision to stay home, thinking she would be in agreement with me. Instead she said, "You should go. Remember those dreams you had of Africa? Go scout out the land."

I thought about it and felt that maybe she was right. I should go. I called Ron and told him I would accompany him.

Three weeks later, I was looking out over the Sahara Desert from the window of a British Airways Boeing 747. I was about to land in Africa!

The Griner family less than two years after returning from living in Costa Rica. Our daughters from left to right: Lacy, Danielle and Bethany.

PART II | THE WINDS OF AFRICA

"The mind of man plans his way, But the LORD directs his steps." Proverbs. 16:9 NASB

CHAPTER 6 | WIND IN MY SAILS

We arrived in the capitol city of Lusaka, Zambia after a demanding 24 hours of almost nonstop travel. It was six o'clock in the morning and we were exhausted, but excited. I grabbed my bag and proceeded to the stairs that were wheeled to the plane door. Though we were told it was the beginning of the rainy season, this morning was surprisingly clear, cool and bright. I was in Africa.

Stepping out into the early morning air, everything seemed intense. The sky was extremely blue, more so than I had ever seen. The air was filled with the aroma of fresh cut grass and the trace smell of jet fuel. The fields surrounding the runway stretched out indefinitely. The only thing on the blue horizon was an occasional plume of smoke from a grass fire. This was no LAX (the Los Angeles International Airport).

We made our way across the tarmac and toward the baggage claim area. After we gathered our luggage, we passed through a lazy customs station then stepped into a sea of black faces busily greeting each other.

On the way to our hotel, I peered out the bus window at the passing countryside. Approaching town, people so filled the sides of the streets that I thought our driver might hit someone. But he didn't seem as concerned about it as I was. There was obviously a mutual understanding between those in vehicles and those on foot.

The agenda for our trip was to visit the copperbelt city of Luanshya. There we were scheduled to minister in a conference and to hold a crusade near the center of town. The following day, an hours' journey by plane brought us to the copperbelt city of Kitwe where we were greeted by our host pastor. From there we traveled by jeep to Luanshya.

Luanshya was once the hub of the African copperbelt, but in the recent past the city and its people have suffered tremendous social and economic loss. As business dropped and the HIV/AIDS epidemic rose, Luanshya became a ghost town.

When we arrived there, the town appeared exactly that—old, with a few paved but pothole-filled roads and little activity. Many shops were closed and boarded up. Only a few bars and barbershops were open for business. The faded paint of the advertisement signs that scattered the town reminded its residents of times passed.

Our hours during the day were spent teaching at the Bible conference with less than 30 in attendance. In the evenings we held an evangelistic outreach at a soccer field adjacent to the center of town.

When I agreed to go to Africa and participate in the gospel meetings, I had envisioned large crowds and hundreds of people being saved, healed and delivered. Instead, the meetings were tiny and the crusade turned out to be ministry on a broken-down stage with dysfunctional sound equipment to 500 screaming children. The first time I stood up to preach lasted only about five minutes because of the unruliness of the children. In frustration, I handed the microphone over to Ron and sat down.

Here I was, at last in Africa. But there was no landslide of souls. There was no wind in my sails. It all seemed to be a big mess. The only consolation Ron and I had was that there would be another day to preach. I couldn't wait to go home.

Divine Connection

We returned to Lusaka and checked into a hotel preparing to catch the next day flight back to the States. The following morning, while checking out, I met a woman named Joyce Mabasha.

Joyce was a Christian and a Zambian businesswoman who worked for several years as a manager of the hotel we stayed in. As we conversed about the Lord and my visit to Zambia, she told me about her husband's dream to have a shortwave radio station to broadcast the message of Christ across Africa and the world. She also mentioned that he was presently working for the Zambia National Broadcasting Corporation (ZNBC), the local and national television station.

That bit of information prompted me to tell her that I was also in

WIND IN MY SAILS 45

broadcasting. I told her how my church in the United States had a television production studio that produced and aired Christian programs in our city. Before I could say much more Joyce interrupted, "Pastor Griner, Zambia desperately needs solid Christian teaching. Why don't you air a program on ZNBC?" As soon as she said it, the idea seized me. I responded, "Well, maybe that would be a good idea." She encouraged me to go and talk with her husband and, since I had a few hours to spare before leaving for the airport, I called her husband, Charles, at ZNBC.

He suggested I come right over, so I summoned a taxi and within five minutes I arrived at the broadcasting facility of ZNBC. Passing through their security, I was taken to a small, drab, windowless office where Charles worked.

I stepped in and introduced myself. Charles was a very cordial and joyful man, and we had an enjoyable conversation about Christian broadcasting and his dream of starting a Christian shortwave radio station. I didn't think much of his aspirations though, because all I could contemplate was how much such a venture would cost. Though he was full of zeal, it seemed improbable that a man of his station in life would be able to accomplish such things. Being polite, I prayed with him and left it at that.

Of course, I had no thought that within two years he would be building *Christian Voice*, a shortwave radio station of 75,000 watts that would broadcast all the way into China and Russia. And little did I know that I would have one of the charter programs—*Power in Reality*. My goal for the moment was simply to explore the concept of broadcasting my own program on Zambian television. When I left his office, I had signed a broadcast contract with ZNBC to air a 30-minute weekly program. I left energized.

When I got back to the hotel and told Ron what had happened, he laughed in disbelief. Heads spinning, we rushed to catch our plane home. Was it possible that what seemed to have been a disastrous trip was turning out to be the beginning of a whole new ministry?

Broadcasting in Zambia

Arriving home, I immediately began to produce Bible teaching videos and have them converted to PAL, the broadcasting format suited for

Africa. Within a month, I was on Zambian television. I called the program *Power in Reality* because I wanted to convey the reality of Christ in contrast to the deadness of religion.

Letters began pouring in from all over Zambia, plus others from some of the border towns of surrounding countries. So many letters came in that I had to organize a special team to answer the mail on a weekly basis. We also sent hundreds of sermon tapes free of charge to anyone who requested them. It was almost a full-time job keeping up with it all. There were many reports of salvations, healings and people being encouraged in Christ.

Much of the mail I received also came from African pastors who had been encouraged through my broadcast. They particularly liked my emphasis on having a living, personal relationship with the Holy Spirit rather than dead religion.

After a year of broadcasting in Africa and seeing its positive impact, I felt inclined by the Lord to hold a series of special meetings for the pastors and leaders of Zambia.

What God had been doing through the broadcasts was humbling. Even more so was the idea of ministering to the leaders of the African church. I felt this was an opportunity being given to me by the Lord—a sacred trust to minister to His shepherds.

I knew that to touch them was in essence to touch the African church for whom Christ died.

The Favor of the Lord

The Lord was fulfilling His word that if I would hoist up my sails, He would fill them. The way that everything unfolded, from my first trip to Africa, to the people He had brought along my path and the ministry He had given me, was surely all a work of His hands. God was doing something.

The pastor's conference was to be held at the Pamodzi Hotel in Lusaka. I used my television program *Power in Reality* to advertise the event, specifically inviting pastors and church leaders to attend. I thought that if 200 people showed up, I would be on the right track.

While I was finishing my preparations for the conference, I received a call from the Zambian Secretary of State.

I was surprised when I answered the phone. In a thick African accent, the man expressed that the Zambian government had heard of the pastor's conference I was to hold. He was calling on behalf of the newly elected Christian president to say that they were happy I was coming and would like to help in any way they could. They requested to pick us up from the airport. He also told me that they had a national committee of Christian clergy who were assigned to assist ministries like ours that were coming into the country. I was grateful to the Zambian government and thanked the Secretary of State for his call. I told him I looked forward to meeting him when I arrived.

Things seemed to be getting out of hand. I mean, I was no VIP; just a pastor from a small church in Nevada. Now I was getting calls from the government of a nation.

When we landed in Lusaka a month later, the president's staff was there to meet us. They walked us right through customs without any formalities to a waiting car and sped us away to our hotel. The following morning we were invited to the Zambian State House where we had coffee and tea with the president and a time of prayer. He gave us his blessing and encouraged us to evangelize his country saying he would help us in however he could.

Though all the attention was remarkable, it also made me a little uncomfortable. I wanted to say, "Excuse me, I think you have the wrong guy." But I held my tongue. I knew this was the Lord. He was putting wind in my sails and I only needed to enjoy the ride.

The morning I arrived at the location of the conference there was a line of pastors signing up at the registration table. I approached the table, and a man intercepted me asking if there was anything he could do for me. The man was Peter Ndhlovu, an African pastor who served on the president's committee to assist ministries that came to Zambia. He was appointed to be our personal assistant while we were in the country. With his white clerical collar contrasted against his black African face, he was a radiant man. He said little, but was ready and willing to serve us in anyway he could. From first impressions, he seemed to be a prince of a man.

I thanked him and told him I had everything I needed. With a big smile he said, "OK," then slipped into the meeting room.

By the time the meeting started, more than 200 pastors and leaders were in attendance. Worship was provided by a local church and was purely African. This was my first experience with African worshippers and what an experience it was! With all their hearts, they swayed, danced and lifted up their hands in joy to the Lord. Before the worship started, most of them sat in their seats, very quiet and reserved. But when the worship began, they were transformed into dynamic expressions of love for God.

The Spirit of God filled the meetings and I was encouraged to see how the Lord ministered to these pastors in such a tangible way. The Lord told me years before, if I would go to the center of the world He would fill my sails. Now here I was and He was doing it.

Wonderful fruit came from these meetings too. One couple that attended the meetings was so touched by the Lord, that they quit their jobs in Lusaka and moved to the western town of Mongu to pioneer a new church. Today, that church has grown to more than 800 members.

Most importantly, though least apparent at the time, the Lord started to form a special relationship between Pastor Peter Ndhlovu and I.

Pastor Peter and Dr. Griner in front of Peter's church in Matero (June, 2005).

CHAPTER 7 | GOD'S PLAN IS A MAN

Whenever God is going to do something, he always finds a man to do it through. He doesn't look first for a method, or organization, or plan.

God's plan is a man.

Not any kind of a man, but one yielded to the Lord, one who is humble and pliable in God's hand; a praying man, a man like Peter Ndhlovu.

Peter had come to Lusaka from the Ngulube village in the Eastern providence of Zambia. He was saved as a young man under the ministry of a South African evangelist who had preached in his church. Afterwards he was very zealous for the Lord and went to Bible school. Upon graduating, Peter became an ordained pastor in the Reformed Church of Zambia.

The Power of God

Following my first leader's conference in Lusaka, I returned again to Zambia this time to hold my first African crusade in the copperbelt city of Kitwe. I also planned a conference on the Holy Spirit in Lusaka.

The evangelism meetings opened in a soccer stadium in Kitwe on a Monday afternoon with over ten thousand in attendance. Pastor Peter was there also; he had come over with my outreach director to help with the set up. During the two days of meetings he stood at the bottom of the stage watching, taking it all in, but I never noticed him.

By the end of the second night he had witnessed thousands confessing Jesus as Lord. He also saw an old lady that was deaf and mute receive her hearing and speak for the first time in over four years! A little boy that was deaf for several years also had his ears opened! And then there was the lady with a tumor who testified it had disappeared. The crowd rejoiced as a young man with a skin disease reported complete healing. Finally, a man with a terrible ulcer condition in his stomach confessed he was healed and declared he was going home to eat *nshima* (a staple food in Zambia made of cornmeal). The crowd erupted in praise!

Having come from a church that was dead in religion, Peter was captivated by what he saw God do in our meetings. A new determination was filling his soul. He desired to preach the gospel as he saw us preach—a gospel alive by the power of God, with signs, wonders and miracles; a ministry that can only be accomplished by the Spirit of God.

Filled with the Spirit of God

It was this kind of ministry that Jesus spoke about with His disciples before ascending up to heaven. The disciples were to testify of all that they had seen and heard, especially that of Jesus rising from the dead.

Jesus said, "You are witnesses of these things. Behold, I send the promise of My Father upon you; but tarry in the city of Jerusalem until you are endued *with power* from on high" (Luke 24:48–49).

And again Jesus said:

> "For John truly baptized with water, but you shall be baptized with the Holy Spirit not many days from now. . . . You shall receive power when the Holy Spirit has come upon you; and you shall be witnesses to Me in Jerusalem, and in all Judea and Samaria, and to the end of the earth" (Acts 1:5,8).

The early Church was not only *born* of the Spirit, but also required to wait until it was *empowered* by the Spirit, for only then would it be able to fulfill its great commission.

The disciples followed the instruction of Jesus and indeed were endued (literally *clothed*) with power from on high. They received a new potential to bear witness to what they had seen and heard. In this power they went on to evangelize their whole known world, see the lame walk (see Acts 3:2–10) and preach the gospel with boldness (see Acts 4:13–20). Only because of being filled with the Spirit of God were the disciples able to accomplish the mission and be able to say like Jesus:

"The Spirit of the LORD is upon Me, because He has anointed
Me to preach the gospel to the poor; He has sent Me to heal
the brokenhearted, to proclaim liberty to the captives and
recovery of sight to the blind, to set at liberty those who are
oppressed" (Luke 4:18).

It was this same empowerment of the Spirit that Peter longed for in
his own ministry.

Peter's Experience

After the Kitwe meetings, we flew to Lusaka to hold a conference
on the Holy Spirit at the Mulungushi Conference Center. In the course
of the meetings the Lord had me call Peter to come up on the stage. I had
been teaching how the Lord desires to fill us with his presence according
to Ephesians 5:18, "And be not drunk with wine, wherein is excess; but
be filled with the Spirit . . ."

When those attending the conference—who were from all sorts of
church backgrounds—saw Peter come forward dressed in his white, clerical
collar, all heads turned. Being filled with the Spirit was not a part of
Peter's denominational tradition and everyone knew it. I knew it also, yet
during the time that he served with us I recognized he was becoming
increasingly hungry for more of God.

When I told Peter that I felt led to pray for him to be filled with the
power of the Holy Spirit, he acknowledged his willingness. I laid my
hands upon him and prayed while several thousand people looked on.
There was nothing seemingly special about the prayer and no physical
manifestations of any kind resulted. It seemed by all appearance that
nothing had happened. Yet something had happened; not so much then,
but as I would learn later, Peter had been overwhelmed in the presence of
the Spirit when he had attended our first leader's conference months
before at the Pamodzi Hotel. Now he was getting a booster prayer. God
was preparing His man.

A Servant

In the months that followed, Peter diligently served alongside of us,
participating in all our outreaches in the country and offering his assis-

tance in any way he could. No one was more of a servant to us than he was. He worked tirelessly to make the necessary arrangements for every ministry opportunity we had, asking nothing in return. I can confidently say, after working closely with Pastor Peter, all that he did was unto the Lord. He cared more about that than any approval of man.

I particularly remember going to Chipata to do a crusade. When I arrived, the platform was built but the sound equipment was not fully set up. I found this man Peter working feverishly to make things ready. Sweat running down his face; he was under the stage arranging electrical cords. His commitment to me was unwavering, always working and never a complaint. This is one of the special qualities of the man God uses.

In those early days, I didn't know who Peter would become in the Lord. I appreciated him and knew he was a helpful hard worker, and a loving pastor, but I had no understanding that this man would become my co-worker, and that soon he would be used of the Lord to start a fresh church planting movement that would sweep across Zambia, affecting thousands, and that I would start an organization to help him accomplish his work. This all remained hidden, waiting to unfold in the timing of God.

The Holy Spirit Conference at the Mulungushi.

Chapter 8 | Backlash of Tradition

*A*t home in Nevada, I received a telephone call. It was Peter and he was electric.

"Peter, what's going on?" I asked.

For the next half hour he told me about how he had conducted his own gospel crusade and prayed for the sick, just as he had seen me do in my outreaches. "Pastor," he said, "there was a man who was blind and God healed him. After we prayed for him, he could see perfectly!"

He continued telling me about people who were delivered from demon possession and from witchcraft, and how many people confessed Christ as their Savior. I was blessed by his story; still it had not yet become clear to me that Peter had been thoroughly filled with the Holy Spirit.

The following summer I returned to Zambia and ministered in Peter's church in Matero. I had preached there several times before but this time I noticed something different. The members of his congregation were lifting up their hands in praise to God. In times past they had been more like wooden sticks. Now there was an obvious freedom. Then I understood. Peter had not only been filled with the Spirit, but he had brought the experience to his church. Spirit filled life had come to his Matero church.

But trouble was just down the road.

Peter's own church continued to grow, though there was some resistance to the new message and experience he brought. Several of his elders complained that the order of tradition was being substituted with spontaneous loud praying and worship with what they considered the unsightly practice of lifting hands. It was also deemed unseemly that some would burst out into spiritual praise language during the preaching.

When news of the complaints made against Peter reached the regional leaders of the denomination, they called for an account of Peter's teaching and accused him of heresy in heated debates that hit the local newspapers. To make matters worse, denominational leaders reacted to the situation by withholding his salary with the intent of driving him out of the pastorate and out of the church.

Bringing charges to discredit him, they also took him to civil court, but the judge threw the charges out as unfounded. In the meantime, several other key pastors in his denomination were also filled with the Holy Spirit.

Over the next few years, Peter and eight other pastors continued to meet with the leaders of their denomination to try and find agreement. They met again and again to debate the theology of a Spirit-empowered life, yet to no resolve. Meanwhile, 12 more pastors from the denomination were filled with the power of the Holy Spirit and came to Peter's side.

In the midst of all this upheaval and to everyone's surprise, Peter was elected as the president over his denomination. This caused no small stir and many of the older leaders were indignant as it looked like the whole denomination might forsake the religious order of the church. On the other hand, Peter and the pastors supporting him were eager to see what the Lord might do. But in the end, the institution was unwilling to change. In retaliation, they again took Peter and several other leading pastors to civil court, fighting to have them ousted from their churches.

Pastors Poisoned

Then the situation became tragic. At a church gathering in the Eastern province, two pastors who endorsed Peter and the Spirit-empowered life were served food that was mixed with rat poison, resulting in the death of one of the pastors and the hospitalization of the other. An official criminal investigation was conducted and two men were arrested and jailed. It was discovered that two of the opposing church elders had performed the deed as a warning to the rest of the pastors who went against church traditions.

Left with no alternative, Peter and the other pastors made their decision to prepare to exit from the denomination. Yet before they could resign, the denominational elders met in Chipata and summoned the nine leading pastors for a tribunal. In the end the elders decided that all pastors who went against church traditions were to be excommunicated.

On March 4, 2001, a formal letter was read in every congregation in the denomination informing all the church members of the council's decision to excommunicate the pastors. Anyone who did not agree with the decision was instructed to leave as well. What resulted was an exodus of over 20 pastors and the majority of their congregations.

The Birth of BIGOCA

At the Great Chinese Restaurant in Lusaka, on March 6, 2001, the ousted pastors organized into an association of churches calling themselves the Bible Gospel Church in Africa, or BIGOCA for short. It had been a long season of persecution but now they were free to follow the Spirit of God as never before.

Congratulations came from many ministries honoring the new group for its longsuffering and integrity in the way it exited the old denomination.

The BIGOCA leaders wasted no time in drawing up a constitution and a mission statement for their new organization. The primary thrust of the group was to become a church planting movement across central Africa and beyond. The vision was big and the twenty plus churches that had joined themselves under the leadership of Pastor Peter were eager in the face of a bright future.

But the days of joy were soon dampened in the face of further treachery by the resisting denomination. The old church immediately summoned the police to evict the pastors and their families from their homes. Ruthlessly, they were literally thrown out into the streets. No one thought they would do such a thing. Yet they did.

A Cry for Help

It was very early in the morning when I received a telephone call from Pastor Peter. I knew by the urgency in his voice that something was wrong.

"Dr. Tom, can you help us?" he asked.

He then told me the story of all the pastors and their families who had been disowned by the church. In his denomination, every pastor receives his salary and housing from the denomination itself. The church owns and controls everything. So when the pastors were excommunicated, they lost their buildings, their homes and their entire livelihood. They literally had no place to turn to and nowhere to live. They were out on the streets with their families; kicked to the curb by the church institution they had faithfully served for so many years.

I knew that this was a very critical time in what God was doing. I could see the attempt to cut this fledgling movement off at the knees.

In faith I said, "Peter, you can count on me. I will help." I agreed to sponsor the whole group (21 pastors and their families) for nine months at $200 per month, per family. When our conversation ended, I knew Peter's heart was at peace, but mine wasn't. What would I do? I had just agreed to sponsor 21 families for nine months!

Falling on my face to pray, the Lord immediately gave me assurance that the money would come in. Without wasting any time, I got on the phone and called some friends and told them about the situation and the need. I also announced it to my church. By the beginning of the next week, I had over $3,700 pledged in monthly support for the care of the pastors and their families. And without realizing it, we were falling right into the purposes of God. This program of pledges for these worthy pastors (and their families) would be the beginning of a partnership expressing itself as Father's Heart Africa, an organization that would feed hungry children, educate, and sponsor pastors to start new churches across Africa.

In those formative days many in Zambia thought these pastors would never survive. They predicted they would be running back to the old order of things before the year was out. On the contrary, the Lord was doing a new thing. And our financial help was unmistakably part of His plan to launch BIGOCA into His purposes. Today (2005), this fledgling group of churches has grown to multiple thousands of members in over 150 churches throughout Zambia and the surrounding countries. Our partnership has been blessed, and the Lord has multiplied the return on our investment. For that we give Him all the glory.

The first BIGOCA pastors at the intial formation of the association of churches with Father's Heart Africa partner Tom Long (left), and Father's Heart Africa missionary Mike Devine (right).

Part III | The Native Missionary Movement

There is one common thread among these native missionary movements; they are all homegrown. They are the fruit of the seeds of the gospel springing up in their indigenous (local) soil. And it is obvious that in the long run, they are going to outdo their Western counterparts. This is not to discount the Western effort, it was first to plant the gospel seeds.

Grandma has 22 Orphans

The elderly Mrs. Banda (top left corner) lives in constant desperation. She is the sole provider for 22 grandchildren (17 shown) that were orphaned by the deadly scourge of AIDS. This elderly woman has the unbelievable responsibility of caring for, and feeding these children. During our visit, we looked in her kitchen and to our dismay, there was absolutely nothing to eat, not so much as a slice of bread.

Father's Heart Africa, in partnership with local churches, are helping to relieve the suffering of families such as these. Each month we are buying hundreds of 55kg bags of corn to give to the more than 500 families we are caring for. The lady to the right of me in the picture is Agnes. She is a Christian volunteer sent out by Father's Heart Africa to visit and care for families like Mrs. Banda's on a weekly basis.

CHAPTER 9 | THE CHANGING LANDSCAPE OF WORLD MISSIONS

*T*he story of BIGOCA is unique and special but it is not an isolated one. All over the third world, Christian nationals are rising up to proclaim the gospel, not only in their own countries, but in other nations as well. And they are doing it against incredible odds. It is a movement that is destined to change the world for Christ.

While Bad Men do Evil

The Democratic Republic (D.R.) of Congo, like so much of Africa, is ripe for a gospel harvest because it has been so wounded. This nation (where French is the official language[4]) has suffered wars for years, and has never known any other kind of government other than that of dictatorship.

The country was originally colonized by Belgium in a quest to mine its immense resources including rubber and ivory. Since their independence from Belgium in 1960, they have continued to be the victims of imposing influences and warring factions aimed at controlling their massive mineral wealth. There have been more deaths in the D.R. Congo than in any war since World War II – some 3.3 million between 1998 and 2002 alone.[5] The suffering has been relentless.

D.R. Congo is a vast country, two-thirds the size of Western Europe, with a population of 50 million. Though the nation is extremely rich in diamonds and minerals, and it is estimated that it has enough hydroelectric potential to supply 1/5 of the world's energy needs, the people are still desperately poor. They want peace, they want to eat, they want health, but the fraud and warring factions have robbed them. Even today, while D.R. Congo still lacks the infrastructure to provide its people with food, clean water, health care and education, the theft of resources continues. They are wounded, but despite the difficulties, there is a new move of the Spirit of God.

God's Answer

It is into this world of brokenness that men like Pastor Lamba Lamba and his Come and See churches are bringing hope. While bad men do evil, good men born of the Spirit of God are rising up to bring the life-giving message of the gospel.

For eighteen years, this quiet and gracious man, Pastor Lamba Lamba, has worked in the southern D.R. Congo planting the Come and See network of churches. With little or no help from the outside, his effort has established over 600 churches, with more being planted yearly.

In the face of terrible poverty and unrest, the Come and See churches are proclaiming liberty and life in the name of Jesus Christ. They are proclaiming 'Jesus is the answer' and teaching their people how to live righteously while at the same time, teaching them the principles of biblical prosperity. The result is a change in thinking and a lifting in life. The poor and dispossessed are being saved and encouraged to believe God for a better life; and it is happening. Slowly, but surely.

While visiting the church this past year, I met a family that told me how from nothing, the Lord had brought them into a prosperous apparel business. At their Come and See church, the pastor had taught them the principles of biblical stewardship. The messages inspired them to do something about their lives. They believed that the Lord wanted to not only give them heaven in the sweet by-n-by, but to help them now with food on the table and shoes on their feet. Taking the words of their preacher to heart, they prayed, saved some money and began to make monthly trips to the Middle Eastern city of Dubai buying at discount and then returning to sale for a profit. The Lord is blessing them and at the same time they are now able to help finance the gospel among their own people. Such is the power of the gospel in a willing heart.

The Come and See Church

In my recent trips to the D.R. Congo, I have been encouraged to see a people yearning for the Lord. I have never been any place where, as

I walked out on the streets in the early morning, I saw people in their doorways reading Bibles. It was a thrilling sight.

Neither have I ever been to a church like the Come and See church in Lubumbashi. This homegrown Congolese church, overseen by Pastor Lamba Lamba, was filled by 6 A.M. with thousands of God-seekers. This was hours before the service was to officially commence. The old building was filled to capacity with about five thousand, and was surrounded by another thousand precious saints listening through the doorways and open windows. The sound equipment was surely on its last leg, yet these folks sang and danced, they prayed and gave testimonies, and no one had to compel them or push them to participate. They were people hungry for God. They freely lifted up their voices in one great concert of prayer and praise. And then the pastor exhorted them that they could believe God for a better life. The service went on into the afternoon, a glorious thing to behold.

Co-Equals in the Work of God

I had come to Lubumbashi at the invitation of Pastor Lamba Lamba and other pastors of the city to assist them in a gospel crusade. We knew from our initial meeting though, that this was to be a joint venture—a partnership. These people were eager for us to help; however it was obvious that they were also very capable of doing the ministry themselves.

As I have already mentioned, Pastor Lamba Lamba's group alone had a network of over 600 churches with a leadership structure that was effectual and strong, caring for many thousands of people across the D.R. Congo and into other countries as well.

By the time our semi-truck arrived in Lubumbashi with sound equipment, 50 KW electric generator and staging, the pastors had taken care of all the administrative tasks. Everything was in place. Teams had been trained for intercession and follow up, the meetings advertised, and the venue secured. It was a massive effort by hundreds of churches.

The first night of the crusade I stepped on the stage to an audience of over 100,000 attentive Africans. The following night the crowd was even larger. And each night I shared the platform with my Congolese brothers, together we preached and prayed for the masses.

Normally, in a large crusade such as this, the only one who would preach and pray for the people would be the star evangelist. But I learned a long time ago that the Lord wants a team effort and not a star. He is the star. Besides, the pastors of Lubumbashi didn't need a foreign evangelist from the West to preach their crusades. Anyone of a half dozen evangelists could have preached with the same results.

It is into this climate of the emerging national church and its leaders that I have come to understand my job. It is to help facilitate the ministry of the gospel among them. I must, with all my resources and gifting, get under what the Lord is doing among them and lift them up. That includes honoring local ministers as co-laborers in the work of God. When I share the ministry and promote my brothers in this way, I am promoting

Steve Storey preaching in Congo

the kingdom of God and the Lord is pleased. This is the heart of the new day in world missions.

When the crusade finally came to a close, it was reported that over 80,000 decision cards had been collected from people confessing Jesus as Lord and Savior. Only God knows the eternal fruit born during those days. One thing is for certain though; it would not have happened if we had not had a mutual partnering with the churches of Lubumbashi. At the end of the day the real heroes were the local pastors and their workers. That's why there is hope for Africa.

The Native Missionary Movement

More than the prosperity of the saints in an apparel business, or the success of the crusade in Lubumbashi, the great story is the raising of the national church as God's answer to a sin sick world. It is the story of new leadership taking its place to reach the world for Christ. And they are doing it. This *surge*, called by some the native missionary movement, is on. Everywhere church planting movements are springing up, some with 20 churches, some with 400, and some with thousands.

The leaders of these movements are not waiting to be lead along by

Western missionaries either. They have already been saved and filled with the Spirit. Like in the book of Acts, they are rising up and going to the ends of the earth to win the lost, heal the sick and plant churches for the glory of God. They are the new force of Spirit filled Christianity springing up out of native soil.

These national Christians have come of age, they have embraced the great commission, and they are taking the *lead*. According to studies conducted by missions leader and author, Patrick Johnstone, "in 1960, non-Western evangelicals were around half as numerous as those in the West; in the year 2000, they [were] 4 times, and in 2010, [will be] 7 times as numerous." [6]

Johnstone also cites Singapore as the most missionary-minded church in the world in terms of the number of missionaries sent out for every one thousand Christians. [7]

The national church movement of China is also phenomenal. While living in the shadow of the Iron Curtain, it grew to well over 100 million Christians. Though Western missionaries sowed the original seed of the gospel in times past, Chinese Christians have been taking the gospel into their own country through networks of underground home churches. The reports of what the Lord is doing are awesome.

The same kind of progress is happening in Africa as well. Missionaries in Zambia say that the greatest growth has taken place in the last five years through the planting of hundreds of churches.

In 1986, the town of Serenje had 25 Baptist churches. Today, there are 123. "I have no idea why this is happening," says Thomas Waddil, missionary with the Southern Baptists. "We have no strategy for church growth, it just happens through a series of divine coincidences. The Zambian Christians start the churches; we tell them not to wait for us. They have caught the vision, and we see the result: growth." [8]

Frank Kilpatrick, president of a theological school in Lusaka, says, "The churches grow because the local Christians have a clear vision for church planting and evangelization." [9] More and more, this is proving to be true. Like a relay race, the runner has handed off the baton for the next leg of the race. National Christians are running—and they are running to win.

Meanwhile in North America, it is estimated that as many as 90%

of Protestant churches have no direct involvement (as congregations) with even one living missionary. The point being, non-Western churches are leading Western churches in terms of outreach. The majority of the world evangelism thrust is now in the hands of the non-Western Christians of the world.

And what is our part here in the West in this changing landscape of world missions? I believe the Lord is calling us to a new place of humility. We are being called to come along side the third world brethren, to partner with them for the completion of the Great Commission.

From Colonial to Partnership Mentality

The surfacing of the third world church as a mighty missionary force has been coming for sometime. A wave of global missions swelled after World War II and targeted nearly all the countries of the world, and for the first time, the United States became the dominant missionary sending country in the world.

Until then, European as well as American missions had progressed primarily through the expansion of nineteenth-century European colonialism. Colonialism was the process by which more powerful countries enriched themselves via social, political and economic exploitation over less powerful countries. As colonial powers sent their people and resources to these distant lands, missionaries came along with them. It was a perfect vehicle to reach these new lands with the gospel. The downside of the whole approach was that the colonial way of doing things infected the missionaries and their agencies. Missionaries did missions in a parental, controlling way, projecting their rule and culture upon the people they where trying to reach. I am not saying it was all bad, only that the gospel was often confused with the culture of the colonizing country.

But after World War II there was the beginning of a transition away from the colonial mentality of ruling over the weaker nations. A spirit of nationalism soared worldwide resulting in countries casting off colonial rule with a renewed desire to control their own destinies.

The work of missions around the world did not escape the influence of nationalism either. Those who had been recipients of Western missionary endeavors during the colonial era, now wanted to take charge of their own affairs. And though in theory this had always been the goal of most missionary undertakings (an *indigenous* Church is commonly thought to be one that meets the *three selfs* ideals - namely, "self-governing, self-supporting and self-propagating") the change from colonial rule to home rule did not come easy for many missionaries and their agencies (if it came at all).

Still, for those that were able to change, a new relationship began to be defined. Instead of a colonial/parental mindset, they developed a partnership mentality. Western missionaries began to relate to their national brothers and sisters as friends rather than as subjects and children.

It was the emerging of this partnership bond between the West and the third world church after World War II that is now becoming the bud of a whole new mentality in 21st century world missions. However, there are still those who go on with their parental and colonial mentality.

In South Africa, I know of a mission agency that has been ministering there for over forty years. They have a large compound where they keep their offices, vehicles, and equipment. All of their missionaries live in modern homes and drive the finest four-wheel drive vehicles. Since they are backed by a huge denomination in the West, there is no shortage of funds for them to accomplish their mission.

From one perspective, their work has been exemplary to say the least. They have established churches and schools everywhere, significantly touching their region for Christ.

My only criticism is that they still operate from a colonial/parental mentality. The whole operation is Western all the way. The work of leading and planting churches is primarily by Westerners through the means of the Africans. The nationals, for the most part, are their children and are controlled in every detail.

Please don't misunderstand me. I am not saying they are wrong. They have done a good work with their methodology. But the missionary landscape has shifted. Something new is happening around the world and if seen and participated with, can speed up and multiply world evangelism exponentially.

Training national pastors and leaders is one of our commitments.
This was the graduating class of 2000 in Lusaka, Zambia.

These pastors gather for a group photo in the township of Kanyama
during our 2004 evangelistic crusade.

CHAPTER 10 | PARTNERING WITH THE THIRD WORLD CHURCH

*T*he modern missions movement started in 1792 when William Carey, a simple shoemaker turned pastor, set sail to preach the gospel in India.

Taken with the reality that there were untold millions who had yet to hear the gospel, Carey spoke with a senior minister about his desire to be a missionary across the seas. On learning what Carey had in his heart, the senior minister chided, "Young man, sit down. When God pleases to convert the heathen He will do it without your aid or mine."

In response to this rebuff, young Carey wrote a little pamphlet called, *An Enquiry into the Obligations of Christians to Use Means for the Conversion of the Heathens*. It was a call to world missions and the use of whatever means necessary and at one's disposal to accomplish the task.

Its message had an immediate effect. Several friends created a missions organization and gathered money to back Carey's proposed venture to India. His message to reach the lost continued to spread all over the English-speaking world and became the road map of the Protestant missionary movement.

In 1792, Carey set sail on his first missionary journey. While nearing the coast of India he wrote from his ship cabin these resounding words:

> Africa is but a little way from England, Madagascar but a little farther. South America and all the numerous and large islands in the India and China seas, I hope, will not be passed over. A large field opens on every side. Oh, that many laborers may be thrust out into the vineyard of our Lord Jesus

Christ, and that the Gentiles may come to the knowledge of
the truth as it is in Him.[10]

Such was the heart of the beginning of the modern missionary movement—that no place would "be passed over." There he spent the next 40
years of his life and endured repeated attacks of malaria and cholera,
impoverished living conditions, and suffered the loss of his wife and children. He translated the Bible into 34 Asian languages, started numerous
churches and mission stations, formed 100 rural schools encouraging the
education of girls, and much more. To this day, his name is still held in
high regard among the Indian people.

What is it that made this great man of God such a success? I think
the answer is simple, he had an undying love for Jesus and the lost, and he
was willing to go. He also had another key element; he had partners to
back him financially.

The thesis of Carey's little pamphlet is still as important today as it
was when he wrote it, maybe even more so. Someone must see the need
to evangelize the lost and then, either go or send. Nothing has changed in
that, except one thing. Now there is a whole world of non-Western Christians who were traditionally receivers of the missionary effort. Now they
are ready to be goers. All they need, like William Carey, is a sender. The
workers are already there and prepared, ready to bring in the harvest as
never before. They are more culturally adept and fit for the task than
those from the West. All they need is a little help. They need senders.
This is the genius of this day of world missions.

God is Doing Something Special

All over Africa, in the midst of the fires of poverty, disease, and
bloody dictatorships, people are eager and excited about the Lord. God is
doing something tremendous. The Lord is moving through a world of
non-Western Christians who have received the flame of the gospel given
to them by the first Christian missionaries of the colonial era. And now
they are the burning firebrands for Jesus all over their land.

Soon, the Come and See churches will be in the Sudan, Somalia
and other unreached realms of Africa. Right now, BIGOCA is sending a
church planter into Tanzania to start a new church among the Muslims.

These national church planting movements are pushing into forbidden realms and bringing healing to a wounded continent.

Jeff Kasongo is a young Congolese brother who is being discipled by Pastor Lamba Lamba. For the past three years he has been a full time student at the Christian Voice Bible School outside of Lusaka while his wife remains behind in their hometown of Lubumbashi selling dried fish on the street.

At the instruction of Pastor Lamba Lamba, Jeff took a leave of absence from his studies and caught the bus from Lusaka to Lubumbashi to serve as our interpreter during the crusade. He was happy to come and worked untiringly to help us have a successful event. He was glad for the opportunity to see his wife too, if only for brief periods due to the intense crusade schedule. Early in the morning till late at night, when we preached in the pastor's conference, he was there, and in the crusade, and in all manner of conversations, there he was. By the time he found transport and made his way home it was usually very late. I thought to myself, what a man of God. Never a complaint. He was truly a man under orders, ready to serve and sacrifice. It is no wonder that Pastor Lamba Lamba is finding such success planting churches with young soldiers like this.

I mention this young man because he is the kind of man the Lord is raising up to carry this great gospel to the ends of the earth. Recently, I received a letter from him reporting that he had finished school and is starting his first church in Lubumbashi under the watchful eye of the Come and See elders. Here is his letter:

> Dr Tom. Thank you for the encouragement you continue to give me in the service of the most High. Also, please receive greetings from my wife. Image though, I am still getting prepared for Namibia. I am planting a new church in Lubumbashi. I took some of the decision cards of the great crusade and some of my members today are the fruit of the crusade. They are really blessed. I continue going after them. Best regards to all the members of your team. Serving Jesus, Pastor Jeff.

I wanted you to see that this young man is doing the job and his future plan is to go to Namibia, in South Africa to plant yet another church. Imagine that. In the meantime, he is taking some of the decision cards he received from the Father's Heart crusade in Lubumbashi and is following up on them. I have to tell you that this thrills my soul because the gospel is spreading. And it is these kind of young pastors that Father's Heart Africa desires to partner with. With our help, these proven young men will do even more for the cause of Christ.

I also spoke to you of Pastor Somwe. This young man, who is also a disciple of Pastor Lamba Lamba, has planted a church in Lusaka, Zambia in the township of Chawama among the often-despised Congolese refuges living there. In a recent letter, Pastor Somwe asked Father's Heart Africa to partner with his church in holding an evangelistic outreach in his compound, which we have agreed to do.

The point I am trying to make is that there are young men and woman who are out there. They are already doing the work. But because of the general poverty among church members in third world countries, these young pioneers find it difficult to fund their work to make Christ known. Hence, they must search out employment in order to provide for their families, severely hampering their church planting efforts. In the D.R. Congo, Jeff's wife works selling fish on the street while he strives to establish a new congregation. Pastor Somwe must also scratch out a living while he tries to reach the dispossessed of his community. If these young men were supplemented financially, they would soon be establishing multiple churches.

Don't think that there is something especially holy or noble in letting them do this on their own; that somehow we might spoil them or hinder God from developing their faith if we gave to them financially. Though spoiling can happen if funding isn't handled properly, God is bigger than that. As are His people. It is arrogant and myopic to think that there is no one who can be trusted but a Westerner.

The Lord has many men and woman of character who are faithful, and who can steward funds righteously for the spreading of the Gospel. We must find them, believe in them and give them a chance.

In fact, the work of God in the earth is always waiting on two things, a prepared vessel and dedicated provisions. Right now there are vessels prepared all over the world. What are needed are dedicated resources. The Western church is being invited by the Lord to provide those needed resources through sacrificial giving. And this is why Father's Heart Africa exists, to serve the church by mobilizing these resources for this end time gospel thrust.

Young men like Pastor Somwe and Jeff can be our missionaries taking the gospel into every man's world. When we partner with our third world brothers, we will help speed up the timetable of global evangelism.

A New Baptism in Humility

The issue of ethnocentricity (the view that ones culture and values are superior to all others) must be dealt with in this final hour of world evangelism. What is required is respect, a respect that believes these third world Christians can hear from God and get the work done. Since this is coming down to an issue of control, which is a sore spot for those of us in the West, a new baptism in humility is called for.

The Lord has dealt with me such that I am able to see that our third world brothers are co-laborers. Since my experiences in Costa Rica and now in Africa, I have esteem for the national Christian. I want to give and to receive from them. I am not their superior but I am truly their helper. This is the worldview that must overtake the church of the West if we are going to participate in bringing in this final harvest.

This is the pattern of God, "He must increase, but I must decrease" (John 3:30). We in the West are being invited to sit at the table of world missions, but not at the head of the table. If we can see this, if we will not be blinded by a residue of parental thinking or ethnocentrism, if we can have a heart to be of no reputation, then we can do something that has never been done before.

The Western church must take more of a supporting role by becoming partners and sponsors of the third world church missionary effort. Attitudes of superiority have to go. We must trust in God, that He can do this great work through our non-Western brothers and sisters. Yes, the Lord can use them with their less than superior methods, and their less than perfect technology (by Western standards). In this may the Lord help us to realize: "But God has chosen the foolish things of the world to put to shame the wise, and God has chosen the weak things of the world to put to shame the things which are mighty;" (1 Corinthians.

1:27). In so doing the Lord will fulfill His promise: "For the earth will be filled with the knowledge of the glory of the LORD, As the waters cover the sea" (Habakkuk 2:14).

Eighteen bicycles for eighteen rural pastors. Bikes help the pastors cover more territory in a faster time thereby touching more people with the gospel.

Chapter 11 | Home Grown

*T*here is one common thread among these native missionary movements; they are all homegrown. They are the fruit of the seeds of the gospel springing up in their indigenous (local) soil. And it is obvious that in the long run, they are going to out do their Western counterparts. This is not to discount the Western effort; it was first to plant the gospel seeds.

But now for the gospel fire to burn everywhere it must be a native fire. In Africa it must burn in the African bush. And the flame cannot be taken where it needs to go by Westerners only. This is because our lifestyle and worldview is often an enormous deficit to the endeavor. Let me give you a personal example of what I am talking about.

I was traveling with our Father's Heart Africa missionary couple, Mike and Aretta and three national Zambian pastors on a trip to the D.R. Congo. As we arrived at the Zambian border we were met by a delegation of several Congolese pastors and leaders. One of the pastors had a church in the border town. They had joined us on the Zambian side to help us process our paperwork and to get our vehicle cleared. Everything seemed to be proceeding without a hitch. After about two hours, we finally crossed over. It was almost 6 P.M. and the sun had not yet set. I thought, "No problem, we have plenty of time to get to Lubumbashi."

But that all changed when I was informed that there was a 6 P.M. curfew and no one was allowed to travel because of a potential of robbery. I was irritated to find that we were stuck for the night in this border town. I can't do justice in telling you what a border town is like, other than it is a zoo of people and activity. I would probably not be unkind to call it a *feeding frenzy*.

The brothers that met us said, "No problem. We have a good motel lined up for you." As we went about two hundred yards and turned left, passing through a gated wall, I knew this was not going to be pretty. Pulling into the motel grounds, our materialistic North American hearts began to sink. This place was not just a motel, but also a house of ill repute (a place of prostitution). We anxiously asked if there might be some other options while trying not to sound ungrateful. They said, "Yes," and so we took a detour back through the zoo of humanity to another part of town.

When we arrived at the 'other option' I knew the jig was up. I instructed our driver to take us back to our original destination. All the while our new African friends patiently watched as our agitation and disapproval increased over our proposed accommodations. Finally, we Americans could not contain ourselves. We broke out into a chorus of complaint. It was a meltdown. I cannot tell you how we howled. But the three brothers that had come with us from Lusaka didn't breathe a word. And the delegation that had met us looked on in silent pity.

It is true that there were no towels, that the sheets were left over from the previous guests and that there was every kind of creeping and flying thing. Nevertheless, it was the best available. We were stuck and there was absolutely nothing we could do about it. It was out of our hands.

We checked into our rooms and decided to make the best of it. At least they were somewhat secure. I went into my little room and laid some clothes out on the bed not daring to crawl under the blankets. I slept on top of them. I have been in a lot of places but this was out of my comfort zone. Mike and Aretta didn't even give their room a moment's consideration. They went back to the van to make their bed. If they hadn't used the van, I surely would have. Our three Zambian pastors went to their rooms without a peep.

As the night closed in on us, the noises and smells seemed to escalate. Lying in the dark I dozed off only to be awakened by a knock on the door. It was some misguided customer searching for his lady in the night.

I was grateful to see the sun the next morning. It had been a miserable night. Now I thought, "Where can I get a cup of coffee?" There was no such offering available. Finally, we gathered all our things and were met by the local brothers and our three pastors. They were coming back from a time of early morning prayer bounding with the joy of the Lord. Not us though, we were not happy. We wanted to get out of that place. I wanted a cup of coffee.

At last, we paid the motel bill and pulled out for the journey to Lubumbashi. I felt terrible and I knew we had not been responding properly. I took a moment and talked with Mike and Aretta about our attitudes. Together we agreed we needed to humble ourselves and to make amends. We apologized to our African friends whom, we had thrashed the night before with our murmurings. All along they were just grateful to have a roof over their heads and a somewhat secure environment. What a contrast between us and them!

I am embarrassed to say it, but in reality this was a great example for the case of empowering the nationals. We lamented the conditions. They navigated through them without a whimper. I know they didn't particularly like the accommodations either. Still, it was no issue for them. They adapted. They don't appreciate sleeping on someone else's sheets anymore than anyone else. They are just accustomed to hardships in ways most Westerners are not. Now, I know some would be unmoved by the conditions we passed through, but not many. The fact is, Western types like us have a standard of living, and that standard is a hindrance to the real grassroots work that needs to be done in these more rugged countries.

The Nationals have an Advantage

Let's face it . . . the national missionaries have a huge advantage over their Western counterpart. They speak the language, know the culture and can often live easily among the people they are trying to reach. They can drink the water and eat the food without getting sick. They understand the taboos and can relate to the people. They can sleep four in a bed if necessary indoors or out. They are fully *contextualized*, to use missionary terminology. The national workers fit in seamlessly, increasing their potential of effectiveness and they can do so at a very economical cost.

People from the West can learn the language and the culture, however, we almost always carry worldview and lifestyle baggage that ultimately hinders and increases the expense of the gospel going forth.

I was talking with an African leader not long ago. I asked him about sending some of his pastors to other countries like the Sudan or Somalia to plant churches. He said in African style, "No problem." He told me that if they had the funds they could go almost any place and plant churches. He continued confidently, "We have vision. We have the Word of God and His anointing. We can do it." He also reminded me that what were challenges to Westerners were of little concern for them. Because they were Africans, understood African culture, and could easily learn languages, they could fit almost effortlessly into any African context—eating the food, drinking the water, or sleeping in the dirt. He laughed saying, "You Americans, you only speak English but we Africans speak many languages." He had a point.

CHAPTER 12 | THE CHANGING ROLE OF THE WESTERN CHRURCH

*H*aving ministered in Africa for over a decade, I am well acquainted with our attitudes as Westerners toward Africans. We are thoroughly convinced we can do everything faster, better and more efficient. Nevertheless, the work of God doesn't hinge on the prowess of a culture. Instead, it moves by the Spirit of God through people in an organic way. It moves in their time according to their values, style and method. Though Westerners can add technology, biblical teaching and finances, Christ must ultimately come riding on an African donkey.

When we first started building church structures in Zambia, we wanted the concrete of the foundation laid flat and smooth. That was an important value to us. We bought a laser level to help make this happen. However, when the floor of the building was completed, despite our wishes, it was rough and uneven. We had taught the use of the laser level and explained the benefits of a nice flat floor; still our desires and theirs were not the same. Our African brothers were just happy to have a floor. Whether it was perfectly flat or not, was just not an issue to them. It was only an issue to us.

This is just one small example of the differences that can exist between cultures. Problems arise when one culture thinks its ways are superior to everyone else's. It has taken us sometime to realize that we have often imposed American values on our African comrades, not just in regards to flat floors, but in many other ways as well.

What I am talking about here is what an anthropologist would call *worldview*. Worldview is the set of guiding assumptions that each culture has for understanding life and making sense of it. It is one's perspective on life. The church in the West has operated out of its assumptions of how mission work is to be done. It has also had a view of the non-Western church that, at times, has been less than honoring. Of course, this is a natural result of the Western worldview. With its superior technology and wealth, it naturally sees itself as the teacher and the controller especially in regards to the less fortunate of the world. But there is a problem with this view. It is an encumbrance to what God is doing and more so, a blinding factor.

There is a new opportunity before us, but we must be willing to lay aside our superior mentality to see it, much less to participate in it.

Will We Be Able to See?

The church now stands before the last frontier of global evangelism. It has had the ability to discern the target. It sees those unreached people groups of the world, which according to the Global Research Department numbers nearly 6,500, whose combined population is a staggering 3.4 billion people.

The church understands these groups. It knows how many there are and can give a working definition of their constitution—"a pocket of people identified by their unique culture, language, and ethnicity who do not have any viable Christian witness in their own community."[11]

The church also understands that the only possibility of a Christian witness is that someone would come in from the outside—a cross-cultural exchange. But will the church be able to see *how* this is to be done?

The answer is before us. The third world church is the perfect instrument to penetrate the unreached people groups of the world. In comparison to Westerners, the third world church is already at the door when it comes to culture, language, and ethnicity. They are standing in an advantageous position in regards to world evangelism. They have matured for such a time as this.

Will the church of the West be able to see the instruments the Lord desires to use? Will it realize the need for partnering with these chosen tools of the Lord? Or will it remain frozen in old mindsets of how missions have been done previously? I believe its eyes will be opened.

Cultural Neighbors

Every African village has its own culture different from that of the

Africans in the city. To be honest, it would be a stretch for me to live in Africa, but it would be a real trial for me to try and live in the rural setting. At this confession surely someone will say, "He obviously is no missionary." Well, I am a missionary and I understand culture and worldview. I also understand that the African of the city is more equipped to reach their rural people than I am. They are cultural neighbors so to speak.

If I wanted to minister in a village community, I could certainly go myself and live in a hut and relate to them. But I would still want to brush my teeth with toothpaste every morning. I would still want toilet paper and some privacy. I could adapt, but some parts of my thinking would never change. I am saying there is a better way. I can partner with Africans who are their cultural neighbors. They can go to the village and do the work.

I have told you much about Pastor Peter in Zambia. Father's Heart Africa supplied him with a stage and sound equipment and he has gone out to not only win the lost, but establish churches. Recently, he told me about an outreach he did in a rural village that even by African standards was very bad. The poverty in most rural villages is so extreme that hardly anyone wants to go there including Africans. However, the Lord has given Peter and his churches a burden for the unreached of the villages.

So Peter and his team went to a village in the Eastern province of Zambia. For two weeks they slept on the ground battling malaria-laden mosquitoes and eating a banana a day, or whatever might be available. They would rise early in the morning to pray and seek the Lord. Mind you, no coffee bar was available, no shower, just the cold morning. During the day they ministered one-on-one to the villagers. At night they set up an electric generator and showed the *Jesus film*. The people, many of whom had never seen a movie, much less a film about Jesus, were engrossed in the presentation. As Jesus was portrayed crucified before them, they wept as if they were at the funeral of a loved one.

After several days they set up their crusade equipment and began to preach open air. When they had finished their work, they had established a new church. Even the headman and witch doctor were saved. Leaving a young pastor to oversee the newly birthed fellowship, they joyfully returned to Lusaka. This is the fruit of empowering nationals to do the work in the culture next door.

Anti-Western Sentiment

A final thought for sending the nationals is the rising anti-Western sentiment that is present and growing in the world. Many countries, for political and religious reasons, are forbidding Westerners (including missionaries) from entering their countries. Still, those who are cultural neighbors can get in. A black Zambian has a much greater chance of success in going to Somalia than a white Texan.

We must see the national workers as Christ's missionaries and then we must do all we can to help them accomplish their mission. The world opens up beautifully when we begin to see that God already has missionaries ready and willing. By partnering with them (and I don't mean using them to promote our denomination) we can together reach into the closed regions of the world.

We must face the facts; things are changing. We shouldn't curtail our efforts but work smarter. One way to work smarter is to partner with the native missionary movement. With our help, they are perfectly suited for reaching the unreached and passing into countries that have anti-Western biases. God's national workers can go. They can go with our help into the forbidden regions of the world.

The Vision of Father's Heart Africa

This is the purpose of Father's Heart Africa. We are committed to partnering with the national church to plant churches in unreached areas of Africa. Our method is to partner with carefully selected men according to criteria that include integrity, character and gifting. Once chosen, we work together in a program of support that includes accountability, training and ministry resources such as gospel literature, Bibles and/or transportation. It is a simple but tremendously effective plan and as a result, there is no place that is closed to the gospel.

Malnutrition is epidemic among the children of Zambia. Father's Heart is there to provide vitamin enriched soya to the hungry.

Josef cooking up a 55 gallon drum of vitamin enriched soya for the children.

PART IV | SAVE THE DYING

"Deliver *those who* are drawn toward death, and hold back *those* stumbling to the slaughter. If you say, "Surely we did not know this", Does not He who weighs the hearts consider *it?* He who keeps your soul, does He *not* know *it?* And will He *not* render to *each* man according to his deeds?" Proverbs 24: 11–12

Time is short! The body of another deceased is taken by relatives in a pick-up truck to the cemetery.

This is Stella who is 20 years old, and has 13 orphans to care for and feed.

Children taking care of children.

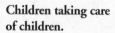

CHAPTER 13 | TIME IS SHORT

*T*hatched straw roofs, round mud huts, animals roaming freely; women sweeping the ground around the hut or gardening in an adjacent field with a baby slung over their backs—this is the African scene. What might appear as a quaint, simple life is in reality a picture of human suffering. In each village and for each person, night and day yield a struggle to provide food for self and family. Seldom is there enough.

Like many African nations, Zambia suffers under the crippling hand of poverty and with it, the starvation of its people. It is estimated that 80 percent of the population in rural Zambia lives below the poverty line and more than half of the children are chronically malnourished. While visiting Zambia in 2002, one UNICEF Ambassador said, "The situation in Zambia is horrendous. . . . I've seen hunger before on my UNICEF travels, but never in this way. Never hunger without hope."[12]

What most people don't realize is that of all the African nations reeling under these difficulties, Zambia is one of the worst. The combination of poverty and hunger with the pandemic HIV/AIDS (called the *Ugly Sisters*) makes Zambia's situation one of the most critical.

It is predicted that in the next decade the global crisis of AIDS will result in the death of more people than in all the wars of the 20th century. With only 10 percent of the world's people, Africa is home to more than 60 percent of the world's HIV infected—some 25.4 million,[13] making it more at risk than any other nation of the world. HIV/AIDS has so attacked the nation of Zambia, that one in every six adults is HIV-positive.[14]

Though Africa is a land of great potential, it lacks the infrastructure to deal with a pandemic of this sort. The devastation has already proven to be of tsunami proportions. Already the disease has taken the lives of some 11 million people and that is just the tip of the iceberg.[15]

At the rate this wave of destruction is crashing down on Africa, the advances made in the past 40 years may be completely washed away. Already the collateral damage of the disease has resulted in undermining the economic and political stability of the region by killing many of its leaders. For instance, in Zambia's public schools, two teachers die from AIDS for every one that begins their teaching career.[16]

In light of the current situation, it is not an overstatement to say that time is short in Africa. The continent is in critical condition.

A Generation Orphaned

In the midst of percentages and accumulated facts, we must not bypass *who* the statistics represent. These are the mothers and fathers of the nation, those who plant the seed, plough the fields, provide for the family and contribute to the overall economy of their nation.

As these become too sick to work and/or die from the disease, thousands of children of all ages are left on their own. In Zambia, where Father's Heart Africa has a mission base, it is estimated that more than 1 million children (greater than 19 % of the child population) have been orphaned, and 73% of these by AIDS.[17]

World Vision estimates that every 14 seconds an African child is orphaned by AIDS. This has proven to be the most horrific fallout of the HIV/AIDS pandemic. UNICEF 2003 reports state: AIDS has already orphaned a staggering 11 million children in sub-Saharan African . . . Half of them are between 10 and 15 years of age and have lost one or both parents to the virus. The rapidly growing number of orphans is beginning to overwhelm the coping capacities of families and communities, with extended families caring for 90% of all orphans in the region. In a frightening forecast the report says that by 2010 the number of orphans will increase to 20 million.[18]

When in Zambia in 2002, I met a young woman named Stella. She was 18-years old at the time and lived in the township of Matero. Three years before I met her, Stella's parents died from AIDS related illnesses, leaving her as the sole provider for 13 brothers and sisters.

Like any girl her age, Stella had dreams and aspirations for the future, the present one being simply to attend the primary school in her village. But she cannot. She must stay home and care for the children. When asked how she provides food for the children, "Sometimes we will go into the city and beg. Often we must go to bed hungry."

Among young Zambians, Stella is fortunate. At least she has the home—a two-room dwelling—her parents left behind, providing a simple shelter for her and her siblings.

One of the great tragedies of the orphan crisis is the number of children that are forced to live on the streets. The last count in Zambia was in 1997 estimated at over 75,000. Now, eight years later some have estimated unofficially as many as 450,000. No one really knows. But one thing is for sure, you can ride the streets of Lusaka, Zambia at night and see a multitude of children sleeping in the gutters; anywhere they can find refuge to provide a night's relief from their weary existence.

And it is especially heart breaking to see young girls living on the streets. They face even greater dangers than the boys. In their attempts to find enough food and shelter just to make it through another day, Zambian girls often find themselves the victims of sexual violence. It has become a prevalent local belief that sexual contact with a virgin girl will cure HIV/AIDS, making already vulnerable girls the target of sexual abuse by many HIV-infected men.

The True Answer
The situation in Africa has caught the attention of nations across the world, from the United States and the United Kingdom, to France and Germany. In early 2005, Prime Minister of the United Kingdom, Tony Blair, issued the Commission for Africa, a 10-year plan which urges wealthy nations to double their aid to the continent, raising it by $50 billion a year.

Though there are numerous organizations nobly giving their time, effort and finances to better the African society, history has shown that mere humanitarian efforts alone are incapable of reversing the devastating affects of the situation Africans find themselves in today. For years, literally thousands of charities and non-governmental organizations from around the world have made Africa the target of their aid and effort in hopes of turning the tide of destruction and raising the continent out of poverty. Yet even secular world leaders recognize that aid alone is insufficient for lasting change. Relief work can only be likened to a band-aid placed on a severe wound. It provides temporary relief to that which needs more serious attention.

I do not discount the relevant work of feeding the one that is hungry, clothing the naked child or offering medical assistance to the sick. I cannot ignore the truth of Scripture as it clearly urges us to care for the oppressed and bring justice to the poor. Jesus said:

> "Then the King will say to those on His right hand, 'Come, you blessed of My Father, inherit the kingdom prepared for you from the foundation of the world: for I was hungry and you gave Me food; I was thirsty and you gave Me drink; I was a stranger and you took Me in; I was naked and you clothed Me; I was sick and you visited Me; I was in prison and you came to Me.' Then the righteous will answer Him, saying, 'Lord, when did we see You hungry and feed You, or thirsty and give You drink? When did we see You a stranger and take You in, or naked and clothe You? Or when did we see You sick, or in prison, and come to You?' And the King will answer and say to them, 'Assuredly, I say to you, inasmuch as you did it to one of the least of these My brethren, you did it to Me.'" (Matthew 25:34–40)

That last sentence is one of the most powerful statements Jesus made while on this earth. The way we extend ourselves to care for the one in need shows the depth of our love for Christ Himself. Yet if this be true, what then is the answer to the problems that African nations face?

Only when the compassion of Christ is coupled with the gospel of Christ, can effectual, lasting change occur. It cannot be one or the other. As the Body of Christ we must not focus on giving our finances and efforts to provide tangible aid while neglecting to give the healing salve that saves the soul of man—the Good News of Jesus Christ.

CHAPTER 14 | VIEW FROM THE KITCHEN BACKDOOR

*G*etting to know Pastor Peter and his wife Hildah has always been a blessing. Many times I have been in their home for a meal and have experienced African culture up close. Each time I visited, a Coke or Sprite was offered as an introduction to their home. Then, after chatting for a while I was usually invited to sit down with just Pastor Peter for a meal that typically consisted of chicken, *nshima*, macaroni, and coleslaw. But not before each of us first washed our hands over a big white bowl while Hildah poured a warm water rinse. I am always humbled to share my life with these servants of God who cheerfully give of their livelihood and time to serve others.

Who are these Children?

One thing became curious to me as I continued to visit Peter and Hildah at their home—there were always other people in the house and children in the side yard. I had never really given much attention to them in the past and thought maybe they were just visitors coming and going. But then, on one of my visits, I inquired about them. Peter told me that they all lived in his home. I could not believe my ears. He said besides his own children, there was Kerry, Webster, Laban, Memory, Maybin and an orphan named Elias. He explained what his relationship was to each one and how they had become homeless. Peter and his family had taken them in.

Then I inquired about the children in the back.

"Who are these children at your kitchen door?" I asked.

"They are orphan children," Hildah replied. "We feed them as we are able." Peter told me that a great majority of the neighbors had orphans in their homes and many could not afford to feed them. The situation was dire and so they were doing all they could to help. They fed any that came to their door.

I felt my face flush a little as I began to realize that I had been eating all this time in the dining room, always a big meal, while just behind the curtain covered doorways of that little house were Peter's family of four, six others, and hungry orphans at the kitchen door. Theirs was a different life, a life of leanness and sacrifice for the sake of some hungry orphans. I was deeply touched at how Peter and his family, in the mist of their own lack, were giving of themselves.

While my mind and heart tried to fathom living in Peter's situation, I wrestled within, knowing that I could not ignore what I was seeing and hearing. Though my purpose in Africa was primarily to preach the gospel, I was finding myself compelled to join Peter and his family in feeding the orphans. At the same time, I felt panicked at the implications of getting involved and truly caring.

I was haunted by the thoughts, "How can I be with these people and not join with them in their burden for hungry children?" As I left Peter's home that evening, I expressed that I wanted to help him care for the orphan children. I just knew that something had to be done. For that he was very grateful.

What Can We Do?

From the day I committed to partner with Peter to care for the children, he and I began to pray and discuss the possibilities of what we could accomplish together. The first thing we set out to do was start an outreach to feed children in the needy areas around Lusaka. At that time, prolonged dry spells and erratic rains destroyed crops, throwing the country into critical condition with thousands going hungry.

One of the first efforts we undertook was to help children in the very poor township of George in Lusaka. Father's Heart Africa was able to provide the finances to empower Pastor Peter and his church to feed and clothe over 300 orphans and needy children.

In the meantime, my wife Kathie told me that during her prayer time she had had an impression from the Lord that we should start an orphanage. In typical fashion, we assumed that this meant building an orphanage facility by which we could care for children.

When I suggested the thought to Peter, he agreed that caring for children was a great idea, but confessed that he thought the best approach would be to place the children with African Christian families. I didn't have much of a grid for that approach and pressed for constructing an orphanage. Being the gracious man that he is, Peter went along with the idea.

We immediately went on a search for suitable property and found some owned by the township of Matero. It had a couple of old buildings and seemed to be the perfect set-up. After inquiring about it, the city council of Matero said they wanted to donate it to us for our cause. It seemed the vision of caring for needy children was beginning to take off.

A Partnership Formed

Back in the United States, I continued to travel to different churches, ministering and sharing what God was doing in Africa. On one such visit to Church on the Mountain, a small church located in the High Sierras of California, I met Josef Rousek.

After I had shared about all that God was doing and the miracles that often happened during our gospel crusades, Josef introduced himself to me and asked, "Do you see miracles every time you hold a crusade in Africa?" "Yes," I answered. "Most of the time." Then, just as pointedly, he asked if he could go to Africa with me sometime. He said he really wanted to see the hand of the Lord saving and healing people. I told him I would be more than happy to have him come along.

Less than a year later it happened. We were on a plane together, bound for Zambia.

Josef accompanied me to a crusade held in the Lusaka township of Mondavu, where more than 15,000 people crowded together nightly in a dusty field to hear the word of God. Each night of preaching yielded hundreds of people turning to Christ and confessing Him as their Savior. And there were miracles as well. During a time of ministry a nine-year old boy whose arm was paralyzed received healing. In front of all, he proudly lifted up a Bible with his healed arm. The Mondavu people were ecstatic and Josef's heart soared as he saw the power of God at work.

The meetings were wonderful and Josef was getting a view of ministry he had never before seen. But what gripped him the most was not the miracles or crowds of thousands—it was the scene he saw on the nightly return trip to his hotel. Traveling through the streets of Lusaka, he was accosted by scenes of scantily dressed little children huddling around fires in ditches. Seeing this night after night overwhelmed Josef and brought him to tears. It was simply too much for him to handle. Weeping, he asked our driver where the children slept and what they ate. To his sadness, the driver replied, "The children sleep in the ditches and eat whatever garbage they can find."

Josef's heart was broken as he saw their suffering. He thought of one of his own children living in those conditions. Greatly burdened and compelled to help, Josef asked, "Tom, what can I do?" I could hear desperation in his voice.

When I explained to him how my wife and I were planning to build an orphanage, he was eager to join with us to see it happen.

Several days later, we boarded a British 747 for our return trip back to the United States. As Josef and I talked with each other, he began to share more of his personal life and explained that he was in the mail order business. He expressed that he wanted to use his expertise and business mind to help raise funds for the work we were doing in Africa.

After returning home, Josef called me weekly, and made several trips to visit me in my home. We talked at length about the needs in Africa and how Father's Heart Africa might help. It was a joy for me to have someone who was not just giving a pat on the back, but who was earnestly willing to help carry the responsibility.

In the months that followed, he and his wife, Anne, gave sacrificially and took time to make several trips to Africa with me. It wasn't long until Josef and I began to develop a close friendship and I realized that the Lord was drawing him to be an integral part of the ministry of Father's Heart Africa. The Lord was building a team by which the work could expand.

CHAPTER 15 | THE LORD'S UNFOLDING PLAN

*T*he days turned into months and the Matero city counsel failed to give us the property as they promised. Peter began to shop around for other property that we might purchase for an orphanage. We also talked about what more we could do to meet the needs of the numerous starving children in his community. Though the large feeding outreaches we started were helpful, they were too sporadic in the face of such great need. We needed a more comprehensive program.

In our conversations, we came up with a simple idea. Instead of organizing periodic feeding outreaches, we could offer food on a daily basis from Peter's church—a kind of feeding station. By this we would be able to care for more people, more consistently and effectively. It sounded good, so we bought 55-kilogram bags of corn meal and began to implement our new plan.

When I told Josef about the idea to start a regular feeding outreach from Peter's church, he shared how he had been thinking the same thing.

"Tom," he said, "I was praying and I saw in my mind an African woman cooking a pot over a fire. Children were walking through open gates and I was handing a bowl of food to each child." He also told me his wife Anne had the same thought and had suggested several times that we need to expand our feeding program. The more we talked, the more it became clear that this was the will of God for Father's Heart. We were all in agreement that we should begin a mission-feeding program, and not just at Peter's church, but also at many churches in various communities.

Overwhelmed

With this new direction rolling around in our heads, Josef, being the successful businessman that he is, started to ask questions. "What could we learn from others? Who could teach us how to do a feeding program on this scale in multiple locations?" By happenstance, one of his friends told him about a group from South Africa that was feeding 60,000 children each day in Mozambique and Angola. He also learned of a large orphanage that was operating in Mozambique. He phoned both organizations and immediately received invitations to come and see what they were doing.

Josef called me, "What an incredible opportunity to learn from experienced ministries!"

He and Peter soon took off for South Africa and Mozambique to see firsthand the feeding program and the orphanage.

Arriving first in Johannesburg, South Africa, they learned how once a year, corn and soybeans were unloaded from ships then trucked north to be stored in a secure location in Mozambique. There, the corn and soybeans were milled, then poured into a large machine and mixed with sugar and dried milk to create the perfect recipe to feed malnourished children. The mix was then bagged and delivered to schools where the parent-teacher association supplied the volunteer labor to cook the food and feed the children.

In all of this, Josef could make sense of the operational strategy, but it was overwhelming in scope. He asked himself how Father's Heart Africa would be able to run a program such as this. Where would we get the funds, the machines, the trucks and the people to do all of this? He was excited and deflated all at the same time. And yet the Lord ministered peace to him, giving him a confidence that it would all work out . . . one step at a time.

A New Perspective

Peter and Josef continued on to Mozambique to visit the orphanage there. The small plane bounced in the rough winds, tipping its wing dangerously close to the runway as it landed in the primitive Maputo airport.

Driving through Maputo, the signs of poverty were everywhere. Many adults were barefooted, unable to buy a pair of simple foam thongs. Trash that was piled high on the sidewalk was burning, sending a putrid stench across the streets. Holes were still in the sides of many buildings from the recent twenty-year war. The soil was nothing but red sand. The driver explained that though Mozambique is roughly the size of California, it has only one two-lane paved road that runs along the coast. The rest of this vast country was accessed by rough, remote dirt roads.

It was around mid-morning when Josef and Peter arrived at the orphanage. They were greeted by the staff and invited to their evening meeting. They introduced them as directors of Father's Heart Africa and explained that they had come to learn how to run an orphanage, to which laughter erupted in the room. One person commented, "That is what we're all trying to learn." A couple of the people on staff remarked, "Maybe you don't want an orphanage." Josef countered, "Yes, we do."

With patience, the staff explained some of the challenges connected with the standard set-up of an orphanage: Three times a day the bell rings and the children leave their activities and line up to receive their meal. Because they do not work like the other African children, they do not learn the cultural work ethic. This creates problems when they must leave the orphanage. They don't know how to survive on the outside.

By being immersed in a Western setting, over time the children become quite *Americanized*. Even the English they learn is mixed with American slang. The girls don't know how to carry things on their head. The boys have no father to teach them a trade, how to build a house or even how to grow vegetables in a garden. Though they receive an education, they are not prepared to re-enter the African society.

This causes further problems for their future as well. When a girl leaves the orphanage, meets a man and starts to discuss marriage, the man will bring her home to meet his parents. But because she is not like the other African women, because she does not know how to carry things on her head or is unaccustomed to the hard labor of farming, she is seen as an unsuitable match. The man's parents are likely to say, "Son, don't marry her. She is not like us. She speaks English. She is used to a flush toilet and can't even carry things on her head!"

The same scenario happens with boys that are raised in an orphanage. They will need to go to a training farm or to an occupational school in order to be prepared for life.

Josef began to get the point. The staff members concluded with the mention of a ministry in Zimbabwe that implemented a unique way of caring for orphans. Instead of following the standard set-up for orphanages, they sought to place children with African families. By this, the children would be raised in the African context, learn the work ethic and stay connected to their culture. With this model the potential number of children that could be cared for is much greater and more effective in the long run as the children are not raised in an artificial environment.

Peter knew exactly what the staff was explaining. He had previously suggested that building an orphanage would not be as effective as placing the children with local families. When he had first mentioned the idea, we hadn't acknowledged it as viable. But now we knew he had been right with his initial suggestion. We had come to learn of the challenges presented in the standard model of caring for orphans. Peter's idea was a perfect solution to caring for more children, more effectively. Not only would it preserve the children's African context, but it also would make it possible to care for a greater number of children. Instead of caring for fifty orphans in one building, we could place thousands of orphans with caring families. It would not be easy, but it would work.

A Three-Part Vision

It was now crystal clear what Father's Heart Africa should do. From their visit Josef and Peter had distilled two ideas that would change the course of the ministry.

First, we would start a program for placing orphans within church families; something we came to learn was already happening out of necessity in most of the churches under Peter's care. Then we would subsidize each household with food to help relieve the burden of taking in more mouths to feed.

Second, we would start a feeding program in each community where we had churches that partnered with us. These churches would serve as the means of administering the program.

The relationship that Peter had as leader within the BIGOCA churches provided a key resource in seeing these two ideas come to fruition. Since BIGOCA church members numbered in the multiple thousands throughout seven African nations, we had many families available to offer this opportunity to, along with the leadership to oversee such a vast work. This model would bear much more fruit while ministering to many more children. The Lord was giving Father's Heart Africa a workable plan.

There was another aspect that unfolded besides feeding the hungry and caring for vulnerable children. Many of the BIGOCA churches were developing community-based schools for the underprivileged in their communities. Immediately, we saw a third aspect of what the Lord wanted us to do—come alongside these churches and help them educate the children.

Thus, we stepped into a three-part vision. Through the vehicle of the churches, their pastors and members, we would not only be able to help feed children and place orphans in Christian homes, but also educate them and teach them the Word of God. In this way we would be able to help take care of three huge problems for vulnerable children in Zambia—food, housing, and a Christian education.

The Work Today

From Hildah's kitchen back door came a child sponsorship program that feeds and educates thousands of children each week.

Starting from a simple desire to help care for children, the Lord has given us grace to do that and more. He has been faithful to lead us each step of the way and we have marveled at how He has unfolded His perfect plan as we seek to minister to the hungry and orphaned.

With the help of a growing army of child sponsorship partners, and organizations like the World Food Program, we can report that Father's Heart Africa has been able to provide vitamin-enriched food each week to thousands of needy children. We have also been able to subsidize many families (we presently care for more than 500), who are caregivers to orphans (families like that of the young girl Stella and the elderly Mrs. Banda). Overall, this is the beginning of an effort equivalent to the work that would otherwise have taken dozens of orphanages to accomplish.

Besides feeding, we have constructed new buildings that double as classrooms and churches, and we have also been able to provide materials like pencils and paper for the many schools that are springing up in the BIGOCA network.

And I am amazed at how eager the churches are to do the work.

They are not lying down to be defeated by disease, poverty and ignorance. With our help, these African Christians are rising up in Christ to make a difference. They are saving their children and giving them a future and a hope. Each week many men and women from the BIGOCA network of churches volunteer their time to cook the food and feed the children in our child sponsorship program. Each church also designates workers to visit each family receiving assistance and monitor their condition on a weekly basis. The teachers in the schools are also volunteers. And it is all happening for just pennies a day. It is a beautiful picture of the church taking care of the community, just as Christ intended. "Pure and undefiled religion before God and the Father is this: to visit orphans and widows in their trouble" (James 1:27).

Whenever we have shared with believers how God is blessing our partnership with the African church, many have responded by partnering with us financially. As a result we are being empowered to feed and educate more children, and to send out more church planters than ever before.

"I can't tell you how blessed we are as a family to sponsor three children in Africa," writes one sponsor. "We know that not only are they being fed and educated, but, more importantly, they are hearing the gospel of Jesus Christ."

For less than the cost it takes to treat your family to dinner, a child in Africa can be sponsored and provided for with what we (in the affluent West) so often take for granted. It is just that simple. Truly, for $28 per month, our sponsors make the difference between life and death for a child in Africa.

With your help, Father's Heart Africa will continue to do this important work. As our network of churches continue to grow and community schools are established, they become the *Noah's Ark* that will save a generation from a godless future of ignorance, sickness and starvation. It is our privilege together to be a part of this rescue mission, to partner with the African church to save the dying.

Chapter 16 | The Power of Identification

*O*ne of the many things that have impressed me about my friend, Josef Rousek, is his heart for starving children. It is not filled with sweet sentimentalism or romantic fantasy. It is an authentic anguish of rare and unusual quality.

I can still recall his first visit to Africa; traveling with him through the streets of Lusaka, watching him blush with heartfelt sympathy as we passed by little children huddled around fires and sleeping in ditches. I have often thought, if only more of us would have a heart like his then there would be so much more effectual ministry. Yet, I must admit, my own heart has not always been so easily touched. But when I met Peter and Hildah's precious family and saw the orphans they cared for, I could not help but identify with them. The little children at Hildah's kitchen back door could have just as easily been my children. I became tender.

You know, most of us are generally willing to help people in need, but we typically don't like to get too close. We intuitively know that if we become too emotionally attached, we might feel compelled to become responsibly involved. Hence, we often go to great extremes to keep ourselves free from any real consideration of the plight of others. I am no exception.

Yet Peter and I were now friends. I became very close to him and his family. I saw with my own eyes how they went above and beyond, making room in their home for friends and relatives who had no other place to go. I stood in their home as Hildah gathered food for the orphan children who congregated outside her kitchen back door.

There was no way I could separate my friendship with them from the harsh realities that they lived with. I remember calling Peter once on the phone to inquire how things were. He mentioned that things were not so good and that they had no bread in the house. I said, "Peter, what do you mean you have no bread? You mean you have nothing to eat?" He said, "Yes. We have nothing at the moment but the Lord will supply." I told him I would wire some money immediately. This was no scam on Peter's part. The people in Africa suffer. They go without. They live from hand to mouth.

As much as it would have been easier, requiring less of my time, energy and money, I could have said, "I am called to preach the Gospel. Don't bother me with your domestic problems." But friendship demanded that I make room in my heart to enter into the experiences of Peter and Hildah, and the many families in Zambia just like them. I was compelled to reach for what resources I could find and come alongside to help them. In so doing, the Father's Heart Africa ministry to children was born.

Since I have embraced the responsibility to help, the Lord has been moving wonderfully in Africa and in my life as well. I have since come to the understanding that there is a place of power with God; it is the place of *identification*.

Just Like Jesus

There is no one who has identified with humanity more than Jesus Himself. Though He is God, He became a man and dwelt with creation formed by His own hands. Hebrews 4:15 tells us that there is nothing we have experienced nor will experience that Jesus cannot identify with us— "For we do not have a High Priest who cannot sympathize with our weaknesses, but was in all points tempted as we are, yet without sin."

Identification is core to who Jesus is. Consider when Jesus received the news that His friend Lazarus had died. Even though He, being God, knew of Lazarus' death beforehand, He was still touched with sorrow. He traveled to be with Lazarus' family and shed tears with his sisters, Mary and Martha (see John 11:35). He entered into the pain of loss that they felt. He *identified* with their sorrow.

We see that when Jesus went to the tomb where Lazarus was buried, He groaned within Himself and commanded the stone that covered the tomb to be removed. He then cried with a loud voice, "Lazarus, come forth!" and he who had died came to life.

Identification is a place of power with God.

In fact, all effectual ministry flows from identifying with people, just like Jesus did. True empathy for people in their pain and suffering is a place of power with the Lord. When our hearts go out and we identify with the grief of others, God comes. In actuality, this is a form of intercession—standing in the gap. When one stands in the gap for another by carrying their pain and sorrow, the Lord cannot help but get involved. This is because the Lord dwells with those of a lowly and contrite heart, which is the character of true identification. As we identify with the burden of others, we open up a channel for the life of God to come forth. I pray that the Lord Jesus would help us see this through his loving eyes.

Consider Elisha and the dead boy in 2 Kings 4:29–35. A woman whose boy had died of sunstroke summoned Elisha. He immediately responded by sending his staff with Gehazi, his servant. Gehazi was instructed to put the staff of the man of God on the dead boy, which he did but with no results. When Elisha heard that the boy was still not awakened, he went himself. Finding the dead boy lying in bed, Elisha shut the door behind him and began to pray. He then laid on the child, stretched himself out over the boy's body and put his mouth on the boy's mouth, his eyes on the boy's eyes and his hands on the boy's hands. After repeating this a second time, the boy sneezed, opened his eyes, and began to breathe!

It is important to note that this miracle did not happen through secondhand methods. It required the involvement of the man of God himself. He had to personally identify with the situation. To do that, we see he had to shut the door on everything else and become single-purposed.

Like Elisha, we cannot do ministry on the run. We must turn from every distraction so that our efforts may be effective. In essence, we must shut the door and crawl on top of the dead problem, just as Elisha did. He did not hide himself from it, but instead extended his heart and joined himself with the problem, nose-to-nose and face-to-face. He took the time and energy to engage in the difficulty—and then the answer came. The child came to life.

There has to be a shutting out and a stretching out for that which is dead to live. We must be willing to give of ourselves. This is the call of Father's Heart to its partners. Let's extend ourselves until that which is dying is revived to life.

The way Jesus walked was the way of identification. And, by its very nature, identification is costly. It cost Jesus *His life*. "He who says he abides in Him ought himself also to walk just as He walked" (1 John 2:6).

Peter' s wife Hildah, serving food to a little orphan girl who has also just received some new clothes.

Father's Heart director Josef Rousek serving food to hungry children.

Students in one of Father's Heart 59 community schools.

PART V | THE SUPREME BUSINESS OF THE CHURCH

How we use our money demonstrates the reality of our love for God. In some ways it proves our love more conclusively than depth of knowledge, length of prayers, or prominence of service. These things can be feigned, but the use of our possessions shows us up for what we actually are. —Charles Ryrie

Chapter 17 | For this Cause I was Born

*T*hen Jesus spoke to them again, saying, "I am the light of the world" (John 8:12). This was the mission of Jesus—to shine light in the darkness, "for the Son of Man has come to seek and to save that which was lost" (Luke 19:10).

All throughout the gospels, Jesus continually referred to the reason for which He lived. One of the most remarkable references to His mission took place in John 4:34-35, after His encounter with the Samaritan woman.

Jesus said to [His disciples]: "My food is to do the will of Him who sent Me, and to finish His work. Do you not say, 'There are still four months and then comes the harvest'? Behold, I say to you, lift up your eyes and look at the fields, for they are already white for harvest!"

To this mission of seeking and saving, Jesus was committed at all costs, even unto death. Luke 9:51 tells us that when the time came for Him to go down to Jerusalem and bear the cross, He "steadfastly set His face to go." Jesus knew His purpose. He stood unwavering and dedicated to accomplish the will of the Father. As He said Himself: "For this cause I was born, and for this cause I have come into the world, that I should bear witness to the truth" (John 18:37).

"For this cause I was born." Jesus knew His purpose.

Let me ask you, do you know your purpose, the cause for which you were born? I find it interesting that Jesus correlates His purpose with what He says is ours: "You are the light of the world. A city that is set on a hill cannot be hidden. Nor do they light a lamp and put it under a basket, but on a lampstand, and it gives light to all who are in the house" (Matthew 5:14–15).

He is the light of the world (John 8:12) and He has made us the light of the world. Just as Christ came down from heaven, stepped into our world and revealed the Father's love and salvation to us, He has given us the same task to bear within our generation. For this reason, Jesus commissioned all those who would follow Him to, "go into all the world and preach the gospel to every creature" (Mark 16:15).

Undoubtedly, Jesus connects His followers to the responsibility of world evangelism. The supreme business of the Church is to carry out Christ's great commission to preach the gospel and make disciples of every nation.

God's will is that none should perish but that all should come to the knowledge of salvation. But people cannot know the truth unless Christ's body, the Church, goes and tells them:

> "How then shall they call on Him in whom they have not believed? And how shall they believe in Him of whom they have not heard? And how shall they hear without a preacher? And how shall they preach unless they are sent? As it is written: 'How beautiful are the feet of those who preach the gospel of peace, who bring glad tidings of good things.'" (Romans 10:14–15)

The Commission of Love

It was this call that arrested the Apostle Paul, a call that was the fruit of a deep encounter with Jesus. On that eventful day traveling the road to Damascus, Paul the Pharisee and murdering persecutor of the Church, was changed by the power of God to missionary, church planter and martyr of the faith. Years later he penned the underlying motivation for his life's call:

> "For the love of Christ compels us, because we judge thus: that if One died for all, then all died; and He died for all, that those who live should live no longer for themselves, but for Him who died for them and rose again" (2Corinthians 5:14–15).

Paul had been captured by the love of Jesus, a love that compelled him to give his all to the Lord with a passion to tell others of this great God and Savior, Jesus Christ. It was his joy to make Him known. Paul lived the truth, "that those who live should live no longer for themselves, but for Him who died for them and rose again."

If we look around at modern Christianity, it would be fair to say that not many burn as Paul did for the lost. Why is that? It is surely not that we are exempt from the great commission. I believe the reason for our indifference is that we have not been significantly branded by the love of Jesus. We have not received the true knowledge of God that grips our souls and gives us a new reason to live—for the salvation of the world.

On another note, I also think we have not been significantly impacted by the reality of hell that awaits all who are without Christ. A thought in itself that is a powerful motivation to reach those who are on a collision course with the justice of God. In his second letter to the Corinthians, Paul makes it crystal clear that because of the certainty and severity of the judgment of God upon all people, that all will one day give an account for how they have lived their lives, he says he persuades men:

> "We make it our aim, whether present or absent, to be well pleasing to Him. For we must all appear before the judgment seat of Christ, that each one may receive the things done in the body, according to what he has done, whether good or bad. Knowing, therefore, the terror of the Lord, we persuade men." (2 Corinthians 5:9-11)

It was Paul's love and this reality of the impending judgment of God that compelled him to proclaim, "Necessity is laid upon me; yes, woe is me if I do not preach the gospel" (1 Corinthians 9:16). The man knew something and it kept him from just drifting in life. He had seen Jesus and he could do nothing but tell others of the great love he had experienced. He knew why he was born into the kingdom of God.

Paul's life speaks to us that we must also live closer to the Lord, understanding what the will of God is. We must, like Paul, be gripped with the love of Jesus and His mission. If we are not gripped, we will be lukewarm ultimately wasting our days, years and lives. May the reality of

Scripture ring in our souls, "for the Son of Man has come to seek and to save that which was lost" and "he who wins souls is wise" (Proverbs 11:30).

It is only as we live in the light of His love with the end in view (for ourselves and others), that we will be kept from selling our birthright for this moment of temporal pleasure. In these modern times, it's easy to become so self-absorbed with ourselves that we lose touch with the sanctifying power of our ultimate impending encounter with God: "For we must all appear before the judgment seat of Christ." Then, like Paul, we will persuade men.

All for the Call

The novel *Schindler's List*, by Thomas Keneally, tells the story of Oskar Schindler, a German war profiteer who used his position and wealth as a factory owner, to rescue Jews from the horrors of the Nazi concentration camps. In one of the final scenes of the book, the war is coming to a close and Schindler knows he must flee for his life. Yet before doing so, he gives a farewell speech to those he has saved from the furnaces of Auschwitz. In that speech he reminds them of his own struggles: "I have done everything and spent every effort in getting you additional food . . ." and "I shall continue doing everything I can for you . . ." History has since recorded there were never more sincere words of truth in a man's mouth. At the peril of his own life and at the cost of all he had, Schindler saved over a thousand Jews. This man gave his all to save a people. He did it as a duty of humanity.

The question is, shouldn't we as Christians give our all to save a world? Shouldn't we, who have the love of Jesus and the message of eternal life, be saying with Schindler, "I have done everything and spent every effort" and "I shall continue doing everything I can . . ." ?

Like Schindler, we have the opportunity to give of ourselves, including our material possessions, to ransom men and women not from the horrors of an Auschwitz death camp, but from the horrors of an eternity in hell. God give us a new grasp of hell and the real possibility that most people are going to go there, until we make every effort to reach them for Christ saying, "I have done everything and spent every effort" and "I shall continue doing everything I can . . ."

CHAPTER 18 | WHY DO I HAVE SO MUCH?

*T*he years between 1941 and 1945 changed Americans. During World War II, the nation was unified under one clear, strong purpose—to save the world from the works of Hitler and Nazi Germany.

Many who lived during this intense time of our nation's history can testify of the many small ways that ordinary American families supported the work of their nation and their fathers and sons who fought overseas. What could be recycled or conserved was. Nothing went to waste. Households collected kitchen grease because the glycerin in it could be recycled and used to make explosives. Scrap metal and tin foil, even gum wrappers, were collected to recycle for the war effort. A popular billboard at the time read, "Is this trip necessary?" reminding motorists to conserve fuel for the war. When people did drive they did so slowly, as to save wear on the tires and conserve fuel, all to contribute to the war effort.

In light of the battle, Americans altered their personal lifestyles. Everyone contributed in one way or another. Though there were shortages of certain foods and goods, the people endured willingly because of the greater cause. They lived in the reality that there was a battle at hand, however distant, and it must be won. It was not the time to sit back and relax. In this way, they identified with those who were serving in a distant land on the frontline of battle.

Today, the same must be true of us. In order to see lasting change come to Africa through the strength of its national pastors and churches, we must awake, recognize the battle we are in and identify with our brothers and sisters in their need.

People of God, we are in wartime. A battle for the souls of men rages all around us. Now is the time to love not "in word or in tongue, but in deed and in truth" (1 John 3:18). May we know the scarifical love of Jesus:

> "By this we know love, because He laid down His life for us. And we also ought to lay down our lives for the brethren. But whoever has this world's goods, and sees his brother in need, and shuts up his heart from him, how does the love of God abide in him?" (1 John 3:16–17)

Asleep During Harvest

Our lighthearted response to the reality of thousands who perish daily without knowing Christ and the suffering which plagues thousands of Africans, portrays that we do not think it is wartime. Our eyes are turned on ourselves rather than on others. We need to take the admonition of Paul, who said to the church at Philippi, "but in lowliness of mind let each esteem others better than himself. Let each of you look out not only for his own interests, but also for the interests of others" (Philippians 2:3–4).

By virtue of bearing the name of Christ, each of us has been enlisted to serve a vital role in the mission Jesus left us to fulfill—to testify of God's love for mankind, the salvation from hell provided through Jesus' sacrifice, and to bring as many as possible into the kingdom of heaven before it is too late. Whether we are placed on the frontlines or not, our lives should show evidence of the task we are engaged in, for the souls of men are at stake.

The words of Jesus are even truer today than when first spoken: "Do you not say, 'There are still four months and *then* comes the harvest'? Behold, I say to you, lift up your eyes and look at the fields, for they are already white for harvest!" (John 4:35).

A quick glance at the way Christians in the West live is enough to reveal that we believe time is not of the essence, that there are still "four months more." Could it be that we are asleep during harvest? In light of the great abundance that is ours, our lethargy should be alarming.

Why was I Born in America?

Compared to the rest of the world, we who live in the West are people of great privilege, resource and opportunity. We have tremendous amounts of time and money for leisure, and we are able to do almost anything and have almost anything we desire.

Consider this: If you have sufficient food and clothing, live in a house that protects you from the weather, and own some form of reliable transportation, you are among the top 15 percent of the world's wealthy elite. And those are just the basics. If you were to add some kind of savings or investments, an additional car (in any condition), a hobby, a variety of clothing to choose from, or if you own the home you live in, you are in the top five percent of the wealthiest people in the world.[19]

You may not consider yourself wealthy, but that is because you are comparing yourself to someone who has more than you.

To understand more keenly what I am saying, consider that more than 3.1 billion people in the world live on less than the equivalent of two U.S. dollars per day. World Food Program reports (2003) that 842 million people do not have enough to eat—that's more than the populations of the United States, Canada and the European Union combined. Of these people, one out of three live in sub-Saharan Africa.[20]

In contrast, the animals of the Western world are better fed than many Africans. According to Newsweek magazine, the pets of Americans are "living longer and getting fatter." That's because Americans are spending $3 billion a year on medicine alone for their pets.[21] Think about it, three billion dollars.

For those of us Christians who live blessed with freedom and provision, we must ask why God allowed us to be born here, at this time. We could have just as easily been born among the poor masses of Africa or Asia. But we were not.

Why do we have so much? What is its purpose? Could it be that with this blessing comes a serious responsibility to the rest of the world? We must not overlook how the Bible speaks to us of our responsibility either:

> "If a brother or sister is naked and destitute of daily food, and
> one of you says to them, 'Depart in peace, be warmed and
> filled,' but you do not give them the things which are needed
> for the body, what does it profit?" (James 2:15)

Scripture makes it clear that those who have, should share with those who do not. God desires fairness among His people. It was from this principle that the early church lived as a community in which all had their needs met. Listen to Paul's words:

> "For I do not mean that others should be eased and you burdened; but by an equality, that now at this time your abundance may supply their lack, that their abundance also may supply your lack—that there may be equality. As it is written, 'He who gathered much had nothing left over, and he who gathered little had no lack.'" (2 Corinthians 8:13–15)

If we are able to hear it, this principle speaks directly to us in our affluence. The Body of Christ in the West, particularly in North America, is the one with the abundance who, according to Scripture, must share with those who have lack: "Command those who are rich in this present age . . . [to] be rich in good works, ready to give, willing to share, storing up for themselves a good foundation for the time to come, that they may lay hold on eternal life" (1 Timothy 6:17–19).

Rich Religion

Clearly, the purpose of the great measure of blessing that God has given the Church in the West is not so we can live gorged with luxuries. The vast resources and potential at our fingertips makes it possible for us to promote the gospel in the entire world.

Unfortunately, our attitude to material abundance has also spilled over into our Christianity.

Ninety-one percent of all Christian outreach/evangelism does not target non-Christians, but rather those who have already heard the gospel and have a number of churches in their area.[22] While 67 % of the people in the world still have not heard the name of Jesus and 200 million Christians live under some form of persecution for their faith, Christianity in the West flourishes as a multi-billion dollar enterprise.[23] Statistics like these confirm that the Body of Christ has, for the most part, committed its rich supply of resources to *itself*.

Pick up any Christian magazine (you'll find a vast selection) and see for yourself. They are loaded with ads for all sorts of conferences and seminars, Christian entertainment, books of every kind, T-shirts, CDs, almost anything you could imagine. Christian bookstores are much the same. In addition to T-shirts and music, you can also find a deluge of

Christianized pop-psychology and the latest Christian romance novels. Everything from Christian debt-consolidation to Christian singles clubs are all prevalent particularly in American Christianity.

As though all of this were not enough, consider all the ministries that pop up in our Christian world. Have you ever wondered about all these new approaches and solutions? There are seminars for debt reduction, weight loss, inner healing and success in life. There are conferences for divorce recovery, addiction intervention and demon deliverance. There is someone proclaiming a solution or an enhancement for almost anything you can think of. You can go to a worship conference, a church growth conference, a prayer conference or a prophetic conference. And all of these are available on video or DVD for a donation. Whatever you can think of, there is a product.

I don't question the sincerity of folks who want to help others. But we Christians of the West have so much time, energy, and money that we can afford to invent a new ministry like someone would start a new hobby. If we can create and market it, there is always someone ready and willing to buy it.

The truth is, we are loaded with dollars and have created this multi-billion dollar consumer industry of Christian trinkets, books, music and services. We may say we don't have money, but someone is supporting this industry and it's not the unbelievers.

When my African friends come to the United States they laugh at the unbelievable array of *stuff*. They can hardly believe their eyes. An African is blessed to have one Bible, and very seldom would be in possession of a book. This is the situation of the majority of the Body of Christ in less fortunate nations.

From our position of extreme wealth, there is only one conclusion: Love requires us to take this serious responsibility of helping the poor brethren of the world so they might not only have food to eat, but also carry this glorious gospel to the people of their world.

Total Involvement

God's grace has been poured out especially upon Europe and America. They are bastions of abundance, both spiritual and material. The wealth at our disposal is a fearful responsibility, "for everyone to whom much is given, from him much will be required" (Luke 12:48).

It is only reasonable that since we have access to the majority of the world's goods and services, we must carry the larger share and do all we can to help the less fortunate, especially in relation to the spreading of the gospel. Scripture makes it clear that this giving to the poor is not simply a suggestion or a good idea. It is a must for the one who says he follows Christ.

Let us not forget. Remember the reason why God's judgment and wrath fell:

> "This was the iniquity of your sister Sodom: She and her daughter had pride, fullness of food, and abundance of idleness; neither did she strengthen the hand of the poor and needy. And they were haughty and committed abomination before Me; therefore I took them away as I saw fit." (Ezekiel 16:49–50)

How long will we Christians in the West continue to live for our own pleasure and comfortable, almost extravagant, lifestyles? Something must change, and it must change in our hearts.

The only thing stopping the world from being completely evangelized is the lack of total involvement of the Church. Now is the time to melt our materialistic idols into gold for the promotion of the gospel to the entire world. For this is the reason we are still here on this earth: "This gospel of the kingdom will be preached in all the world as a witness to all the nations, and then the end will come" (Matthew 24:14).

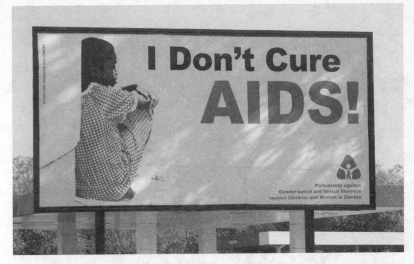

This billboard in Zambia is a testimony to the reality of AIDS and the abuse of children in Africa. The sign is an effort to dispel the wicked belief that sex with a virgin girl will cure AIDS. This shameful practice only serves to spread the terrible disease to the truly innocent--little girls. In our crusades we denounce these practices as sinful and wicked calling men to repent.

The devastation of HIV/AIDS falls heaviest upon the children of Africa. They are locked behind bars of poverty, violence and disease with no escape. Through child sponsorships we can make a difference and save a child.

Father's Heart Africa founder Tom Griner (right) and Josef Rousek (left). The hundreds of 55kg bags of vitamin enriched soya behind them are ready to be shipped to needy and hungry children.

CHAPTER 19 | WILL YOU JOIN WITH US?

*T*o accomplish a gospel crusade in the midst of deep spiritual darkness, or to launch a new feeding program, or to sponsor a new church planting pastor, takes faith in the Lord, faith that He will make a way. Many times, I have returned from a tour of ministry wondering if I would be able to do it again, wondering if Father's Heart Africa would be able to continue feeding so many hungry children and continue sending new pastors out to the unreached regions of Africa. And each time those doubts have surfaced, they have been short lived as the Lord has encouraged me to fight the good fight of faith and to simply remember His Word.

We are not out there doing our own thing. We are moving according to the determination of God. He is the One who has said, "the harvest is great," and "go into all the world and preach the gospel" (Luke 10:2, Mark 16:15). We have taken Him at His Word and we are going. We believe He will sustain His work. Our part is to have faith. Faith to yield ourselves to Him, faith to go where He tells us, and faith to lay hold of the resources He is sending. I honor and esteem an abiding trust in the will of God based on His promises. If He has said it, He will surely do it.

In the early days of the ministry, I learned a valuable lesson about how God responds to faith. I had planned a strategic pastor's conference and gospel crusade in Zambia and Malawi (a country just north east of Zambia). Everything was ready but when the time came to go and to pay the final expenses, I didn't have a dime. I didn't even have plane fare.

I went to my office, shut the door and prayed. Then, in the midst of feelings of helplessness, a word from the Lord settled over my soul: "This is my ministry. Follow me and I will make a way. I will do this work through you." Immediately I was calmed and an assurance that everything was going to be all right came over me. I didn't know how. I just knew it would be. This was the Lord's ministry.

Still, the deadline came and there was no provision. In the past I had always managed to find a way to secure resources for these outreaches. Now my back was against the wall. There were no credit cards, no savings accounts, no one to turn to. Resigning to what seemed to be the inevitable, I resolved to call my team to let them know the ministry trip was off. I knew it would be a great disappointment to them and especially to the African brothers who were anticipating our coming. They had already spent countless days and hours making preparations and had invested what little they had to help launch the project. Besides that, there were unpaid expenses; things like advertising, conference hall rental, crusade grounds and equipment, all anticipating payment upon our arrival. Now I had to pull the plug. It would be embarrassing and I would lose credibility, but I had to do it.

One of the first people I called was a member of my board of directors. Before I could say three words, he interrupted me with, "Tom, my wife and I have been praying. The Lord has told us to give $10,000 for this outreach." I was speechless. I finally said, "Well John, this is surely the Lord because I was just calling to let you know the trip was off." We rejoiced at the obvious hand of the Lord. The Lord once again confirmed His call, and His supply. It indeed was His ministry.

I can't tell you how many times I have said to the Lord, "I can't do this. I feel like wood. I don't have the money. I don't have a word to preach or faith to pray for the sick," only to have the Lord remind me of the story of the feeding of the five thousand:

> "But He said to them, 'You give them something to eat.' And they said, 'We have no more than five loaves and two fish, unless we go and buy food for all these people.' For there were about five thousand men. Then He said to His disciples, 'Make them sit down in groups of fifty.' And they did so, and made them all sit down. Then He took the five loaves and the two fish, and looking up to heaven, He blessed and broke *them,* and gave *them* to the disciples to set before the multitude. So they all ate and were filled, and twelve baskets of the leftover fragments were taken up by them." (Luke 9:13–17)

This story teaches a very valuable principle about faith and provision. I call it the *miracle zone* principle. It goes like this; if you will take the little you have, even in the face of overwhelming need, and give it, then the Lord will multiply what you give to supply the need. There will be enough.

There is a challenge though. The *miracle zone* is a battleground for faith. Think about it, if the disciples would have stopped and considered the impossibility of what they were doing, they would have most certainly wilted in the sight of so much need and in their feelings of inadequacy. After all, they only had five loaves, two fish, and the words of Jesus: "You give them something to eat." What was that in the face of so many hungry mouths?

Nonetheless, the disciples entered the *miracle zone*; that place between the command of Jesus—"You give them something to eat"—and the overwhelming need before them—"For there were about five thousand men."

I am sure they looked at what they had and saw what they didn't have—"We have no more than five loaves and two fish, but what are they among so many? Yet Jesus has blessed it and commanded us to feed the people." As they in faith turned to the crowd at the Word of the Lord, the little they had multiplied to meet the hunger of the masses.

This is the way the Lord works. You know you don't have enough, but you proceed anyway at the Word of the Lord. Doubt and unbelief attack but you keep your eyes on the promises of God. And then, without knowing how, the little you have is multiplied and the need is met. This is what I have seen happen with Father's Heart Africa many times.

Last year we received a donation of dried milk worth over $40,000, but it sat in our warehouse in Bishop, California because we didn't have the money to pay for international shipping. After a while, Josef Rousek suggested we wait no longer. I knew exactly what he meant. We had to act with what we had in our hand. So without the necessary money in our budget, we started the process. We stepped into the *miracle zone*. We communicated the project to our Father's Heart partners and encouraged them to pray with us. In the mean time we ordered a forty-foot empty container and had it packed with the bags of dried milk from our warehouse. We completed the shipping papers. The truck was scheduled to come and pick up the container. The ocean liner was in the port waiting.

Now we were about to need over $11,000 to make the shipment. Some might say we were tempting God or practicing some kind of faith formula. But that was not the case. We were simply acting on our Word from the Lord: "You give them something to eat."

We continued praying and waiting on the Lord. As the shipping time drew near, something wonderful happened. The Lord prompted several of our partners to give the necessary money. There it was, all the funds necessary to send the milk to hungry children. Needless to say, Joe and I breathed a sigh of relief and rejoiced that the shipment could go out.

We know what it is to pass through the *miracle zone*.

Will You Become a Sponsor?

May I ask you a question? Would you be willing to step into the *miracle zone* with us? Would you consider believing God with us to save the dying in Africa by sponsoring a child and/or a pastor? I believe many who read this book will be so inclined. I believe the Lord is calling an army of partners who will join with us to reach the world for Christ. It is His ministry and He will do it, but He always works through people.

Today, millions of souls live in darkness and poverty. They are waiting for someone who cares, someone like you and me, as well as the millions of Christians living in the third world. And together with them, you and I can make a difference. We can save a generation of children, giving them a future and a hope and plant a host of churches that will be lighthouses of salvation in the decades to come. What a great opportunity and privilege that is before us!

And for those of you who join with us as sponsors, one day you will stand before the Lord and hear Him say: "Well *done,* good and faithful servant;" (Matthew 25:23), and "'for I was hungry and you gave Me food; I was thirsty and you gave Me drink; I was a stranger and you took Me in; I was naked and you clothed Me; I was sick and you visited Me; I was in prison and you came to Me'" (Matthew 25:35–36).

Then you shall be greeted by a multitude of grateful people who will say, "Thank you for sending a preacher to tell us about the blood of

Jesus. Thank you for taking the time and sending your resources to help us."

Hungry Children

I encourage you to ask the Lord what He might have you do. For $28 a month you can make an eternal difference in the life of a child. Your help will provide the necessary food, care, and education that some African child so desperately needs. Most of all, the child you personally sponsor will grow up knowing about the love, salvation and hope that is found only in Jesus Christ.

When you sponsor a child, we'll send you a picture of that child and important information on how to correspond with and pray for him or her.

The Multitudes Await

Throughout Africa, God is raising up a generation of national pastors ready to win their countrymen for Christ. As I have said, unlike many Western missionaries, these pastors know the language, understand the culture and live at the level of the people around them. Most of all, they are filled with an urgency and deep compassion to proclaim Christ in their own land and beyond.

However, African churches have little resources available to train and send out pastors to plant new churches. This is where you can help. For as little as $30 a month, you can empower a national church planting pastor to go into some unreached region of Africa.

Your sponsorship will make it possible for him to live, preach the gospel, and make true disciples. Through him the gospel light will come to some dark place because you cared enough to be a sender. What a privilege!

And when you start your sponsorship, the staff of Father's Heart Africa will send you a photo and testimony of the missionary you are helping including where he or she is serving. Then, we will send you regular updates as to the progress of your missionary.

When you hear what is happening through them, your heart will soar and rejoice that the gospel is being preached in the world and you had a part in making it happen.

Will You Join Us?

As the Lord puts it in your heart to join with us in this important work, please fill out the enclosed perforated post card and drop it in the mail today. Or, you may call us at 1-800-873-1753, or contact us through the web at: www.fhafrica.org.

May the Lord richly bless you as you answer His call to reach the world for Christ. And for those of us at Father's Heart Africa, I want to say thank you in advance for helping us communicate the Good News of Jesus Christ to the people of Africa.

APPENDIX 1

QUESTIONS AND ANSWERS

QUESTIONS ABOUT FATHER'S HEART AFRICA

Question 1: Who is Father's Heart Africa?

Father's Heart Africa is a ministry of Father's Heart International, a non-profit Christian organization founded by Tom and Kathie Griner. It exists to demonstrate the practical love of Christ and serve the church in Africa.

Question 2: What is the mission of Father's Heart Africa?

For a continent such as Africa, devastated by the terrible suffering and death caused by HIV/AIDS, it is not only important to provide the basic needs to sustain life, but also to build up a biblical, moral conscience, by which restoration comes. Because of this, Father's Heart Africa is dedicated to serving the people of Africa in a holistic way through supporting their ministries of church planting, hunger relief to vulnerable children, evangelism and education.

Question 3: What are the accountability standards for Father's Heart Africa?

Father's Heart Africa is a ministry of Father's Heart International, a non-profit 501 (c) 3 of the Internal Revenue Service of the United States. The ministry is overseen by an independent board of directors and is also submitted to the standards of the *Evangelical Council for Financial Accountability.* ECFA is an independent non-profit accreditation agency dedicated to helping Christian ministries earn the public's trust through adherence to standards of responsible accounting practices and stewardship.

QUESTIONS ABOUT THE NATIONAL PASTOR SPONSORSHIP

Question 1: Do you think national workers might get the idea that they cannot do the work unless they are subsidized by Westerners?

This could happen, but our approach in Father's Heart Africa is to only come alongside those who are already doing the work with success, leaders who are already proving themselves in the field before we ever come into the picture. The truth is there are many third world leaders who have been planting churches without being subsidized from the outside, and who will continue with or without help. But with assistance they could do their work more rapidly and extensively.

Question 2: Will assisting church planting movements cause them to have no need to give sacrificially of their own resources?

Father's Heart Africa only helps those who are already succeeding in their mission. That means the leaders already have a vision, faith and are using whatever resources they have to accomplish their mission. One group recently sponsored a clothing and food drive to raise money to send out a church planting team. The leaders of these groups know the dangers of becoming dependent on outside sources and continually teach their workers and the churches under their charge to give sacrificially trusting God as their source.

Question 3: How does Father's Heart Africa choose the national pastors it will sponsor?

We do not choose the national pastors directly. We choose the national church planting movements and they choose their own church planters. Our goal is to identify church planting movements who are already having success reaching the unreached in their own culture, or the culture next door. We look for organizations led by men who have character and integrity, men who are biblically sound and not for hire. It is these kinds of men we are coming alongside to help accomplish their vision by providing financial help and ministry tools. We know that these kinds of leaders will require the same standards they live by from their missionary church planters.

Question 4: To whom are national missionaries accountable?

Our relationship with the leaders of a church planting movement is one of mutual accountability. We spend time together quarterly to pray and review all the decisions that are being made. Supervisory elders then hold the missionary pastors in the field accountable. These field elders report back to the senior leaders giving updates as to the progress of the missionary pastors under their charge. These updates are then given to Father's Heart Africa staff for review.

Question 5: Are financial records verified in the field?

Father's Heart staff reviews all financial records. This is to ensure that all the funds are being used for what they were designated. Each person receiving and releasing funds signs a receipt that is kept for review and verification.

Question 6: How are national missionaries trained?

Each church planting movement has its own method of training. In Zambia the candidates are sent to a locally accredited Bible school for instruction. They are then required to participate in a local church for a period of time where they are tested in their manner of life and gifting. When approved by the senior leaders, the candidate is ordained and sent out into the field under the supervision of an experienced church planter.

Question 7: Is Father's Heart Africa a church planting organization or a humanitarian organization?

We are both. Father's Heart Africa is committed to church planting, evangelism and humanitarian endeavors (such as clean water, education, and hunger relief for children).

Question 8: How can I help sponsor a national missionary?

To join with us in this important work, please fill out the atached perforated post card and drop it into the mail today. Or, you may sign up directly on our interactive website at: www.fhafrica.org. You may also call us at 1-800-873-1753.

QUESTIONS ABOUT CHILD SPONSORSHIP

Questions 1: Do you feed and school non-Christian children?

Yes, we are feeding all the poor children that come to us and educating any that come to our schools. In so doing we are touching whole communities for Christ.

Question 2: What do you teach the children in the Father's Heart schools?

We teach the children to read and write in English as well as the disciplines of math, science, geography and history. The children are also instructed in the Bible and required to memorize Bible verses.

Question 3: Do the schools have clean drinking water?

Not all of the schools have safe drinking water. This is a problem and one of the leading causes of death among children in Africa. Father's Heart Africa is committed to drilling water wells in each village we serve as resources allow. The cost to provide a water well is close to $5,000 (2005).

Question 4: What is the role of a Father's Heart Child Sponsor?

The significance of your sponsorship must not be underestimated— you make the difference. When you invest in the life of a child in Africa, you not only provide an education and nutritious meals, but you are helping disciple a nation for Christ. You are giving that nation a future and a hope.

Question 5: How is my gift used in the program that assists my sponsoredchild?

Father's Heart Africa uses your money as wisely as possible. Operating costs and service expenses are essential to run a Child Sponsorship program. Keeping these expenses to a minimum is a priority.

Four important objectives are accomplished with your sponsorship money to ensure that your sponsored child receives help. Your partnership helps Father's Heart:

1. Operate the program that provides services for your sponsored child and his/her school community.
2. Accurately account for all donations to ensure that all monies are applied to the program and community where the sponsored child lives.
3. Process and deliver updates from your child each year so that you can effectively pray for them.
4. Raise up more sponsors to sponsor even more children in Africa.

Question 6: Will I always have the same child?

Occasionally it becomes necessary to reassign a new child to you. Situations where this will be necessary include the child moving or reaching the age of 18.

Question 7: How can I help sponsor a child?

To join with us in this important work, please fill out the attached perforated post card and drop it into the mail today. Or, you may sign up directly on our interactive website at: www.fhafrica.org. You may also call us at 1-800-873-1753.

In the D.R.Congo large crowds gathered to hear the gospel of our great God and Savior Jesus Christ.

Hearts break and tears flow after hearing the gospel.

APPENDIX 2

WHY GOSPEL CRUSADES?

Time is fleeting in Africa. People are dying by the thousands and death is commonplace there. One never knows who will die next. In Zambia, where I have ministered for the past 12 years, I have seen the urgency and desperation. I have seen the fields of unmarked fresh graves. I have heard and seen the people weeping as they bury their loved ones. There is no mortuary to call. They have to wash the body, obtain a casket (many making one out of whatever wood they can find including the kitchen table if necessary), transport the body to the burial site themselves, and dig the grave. This is their life. This is the way it is. It is not unusual to see an old truck with people hanging off the sides, following a pick-up truck carrying the body of a loved one with only the deceased feet in view heading for the cemetery.

And it is these images that have caused us at Father's Heart to push on in Africa. Because of this urgency we preach, and feed, and support church planters to carry this gospel into the slums and villages of this continent. And it is because of this we are involved in great gospel crusades to help bring in the harvest.

Despite the difficulties and possible dangers in conducting a gospel crusade, we do them because the Lord has directed us to do them, and because we have seen the tremendous opportunity. Jesus said, "Do you not say, 'There are still four months and then comes the harvest'? Behold, I say to you, lift up your eyes and *look* at the fields, for they are already white for harvest!" (John 4:35). We have lifted up our eyes and looked upon the fields and can say with Jesus, they are white to harvest.

A Combine Machine

In these great fields of humanity, the churches seldom have the means to do such large events. We come as a combine harvesting machine working with the local pastors and churches to bring in the harvest in each of their respective locations.

In the wheat producing planes of the United States, smaller farms will often join together to bring in a harvester to cut their fields. The trucks come with their big combine machines, unload and cut each field until they are all done. This is what we do. We come with the equipment and ability to bring in the harvest for all the churches in a location.

Yes, these are horrific times of poverty and pain for much of the continent, still, at the same time there is a great door of opportunity to bring the answer, and that answer is Jesus Christ. He must be proclaimed in word and deed until it can be said once again: "The people which sat in darkness saw great light; and to them which sat in the region and shadow of death light is sprung up. Those who sit in the realms of darkness have seen a great light" (Matthew 4:16).

It is simple and effective, this thing called crusade evangelism. It is the right prescription for this people at this time.

Crusade at the Maheba Refugee Camp

After our successful gospel crusade in Lubumbashi with Pastor Lamba Lamba (see chapter 9), our trucks rolled two days to the Mahaba refugee camp bordered by Angola and the Congo in north Zambia. This particular camp was home to more than thirty five thousand dispossessed people from the surrounding war torn countries including Angola, Congo, and Mozambique.

We had felt directed of the Lord to preach there because we had heard that many of the people were bitter and that there had never been a gospel crusade in the camp.

Armed with the special use permits from the Zambian government, our advance team entered the guarded camp and set up the crusade stage and sound equipment. The pastors were ready and everything else was in place. The people were also eager, though transportation would be a challenge for them to attend the meetings.

The first night the crusade was attended by about five hundred. After just having preached to over 100,000 people a night in the D.R. Congo this was a little disappointing. Nonetheless, this is not unusual considering people are so scattered and there is no public transport. Many walk up to 12 miles to attend these open-air meetings. Picture the people walking for miles, with no water or food. They come very early and leave late. There are no lights or places along the way. When they get home it is dark and there is seldom anything to eat. And the next day they must get up and go to their work if they are to eat again. If they don't, they won't eat. Then, if they can, they make their way back to the gospel meetings.

When the preaching ended that first night, as our custom is, we called the sick forward for prayer. As I began to pray, I saw an older gentleman with his hand covering his left eye while trying to see out of what appeared to be his blinded right eye. As I looked at him, I knew he had faith. I could see it on his countenance. The Lord was doing something. I held my fingers up and said, "Sir, can you see my fingers? How many fingers?" He strained and strained to see, but couldn't. I asked again, "How many fingers am I holding up?" Again he strained and with disappointment shook his head that he could not see. I then said, "Sir, we are going to send someone down to lay hands on you. Lord willing you are going to see tonight. This is your night. The Lord is going to heal you."

A few minutes later, after my friend Pastor Steve Storey from Carson City, Nevada, had prayed for him, I saw the old guy again straining to see out of his blind eye. I got his attention and said, "Man, how many fingers?" I held up five. A smile came on his face and he shouted, "Five!" I shouted back, "Yes!" Then I held up two fingers and asked, "How many fingers now?" He responded, "Two." I yelled, "Yes." The people broke out into praise.

We then brought the old gentleman up on the stage where we could do a closer examination of his claim. The man was perfectly healed in his blinded eye. The reality of the healing spread like wild fire in the camp and the next night the crowd grew from five hundred to five thousand.

After many more decisions for Christ, and testimonies of healing, the crusade came to an end. The Lord had shown Himself strong.

Kanyama Crusade
From the Maheba refugee camp we then traveled down to Kanyama,

one of the many compounds that makes up the city of Lusaka. This particular township is an ideal place to present the gospel because it is a very dense people congested area and has a very high crime rate with many witch doctors.

In our crusades we go directly to the people. This is tremendously beneficial in two ways. First, the people don't have to travel to get to the meetings. We are at their door, so to speak. And second, by going to the people the crusade is very economical. We have learned this through experience.

Not long ago a famous ministry from the United States came to Lusaka to hold a citywide series of open-air meetings. They rented billboards, advertised on television and plastered the city with four-color glossy posters, spending many thousands of dollars. But in the end the turn out was very poor.

On the other hand, our crusade in the heart of where the people lived was not only very well attended in comparison; it was less than 1% of the cost.

This is possible because we don't need to hire transport for the people, we don't need city billboards, and we don't require a stadium or television advertisement. Instead, we keep it simple. We go to where the people are and work with the local Christians there. In so doing we are able to accomplish the goal with very little overhead.

In Kanyama, our crusade director Pastor Mutale worked tirelessly with the local pastors and leaders to make the necessary preparations that would net a harvest of souls. He was able to gather over a hundred pastors and leaders to work in a joint effort to touch that very poor section of Lusaka with the gospel. In a dusty field in the midst of the congestion of homes, over thirty five thousand people attended nightly and the harvest was outstanding.

The Lord granted many healings too. There were three young girls who where healed of blinded eyes. Several who were deaf could also hear after prayer. An old lady who had practiced witchcraft was saved and healed. With each testimony of healing, the people were moved with joy.

And then at the conclusion of each night, we called for those who wanted to make Jesus Christ Lord of their lives to come forward. Over the course of the four nights several thousand made confessions for Christ.

There was so much joy that after each night, the people didn't want to leave. They just lingered among the little grass fires, soaking in the experience. It was a sight to behold.

In all, the Kanyama crusade was a rich success. How do I know that? For one thing, reports tell us that many of the churches that participated have doubled in size with the infusion of new believers and to that we give glory to Jesus. Such is Africa, a harvest waiting for the reapers.

Are Gospel Crusades Effective?

For those of us who do crusade evangelism the answer is, "Yes, of course they are effective." But it is not an unreasonable question to ask, "How are they effective?" Especially in the light of those who discount their worth on the grounds of some statistic touting the low number of decisions for Christ that actually became infolded into a local church.

For instance, some of these statistics have reported that only 5% or less of those making a confession for Christ in certain American crusades ever become part of a local church.

Also, in a recent missions newsletter that I read, the writer made this statement, "Of the hundreds of thousands who make decisions for Christ in the evangelistic crusades in the third world nations (like Africa), only a tiny fraction end up regularly attending any church." The article then cited statistics where 1 million were said to have received Christ with only 1/10 of 1 % being found in a local church ninety days after the meetings. From this perspective, the article then drew the conclusion that the "meager" results of crusades compared to the great cost in time, energy and money represented a failed stewardship of God's resources.

I can understand what's being said here, but as one who has held evangelistic crusades in various parts of the world, I know there is more to the story than that reflected in these statistics or this mission's article. My experience tells a different story. After our crusades it is not uncommon that a new church might be formed, or for the existing churches to swell twice their size with new members.

I think that the reason some gospel events might lack in fruit is that a watered down version of the gospel is being preached—a version that doesn't really save. In our meetings we preach repentance and the cross of Christ calling the people to make a whole-hearted commitment to Jesus

as Lord and Savior. We don't give them a *feel good sugarcoated* gospel. We
don't beg them to come to Christ for what they can get. We extol the cost
of truly following the Lord. They often run to our altar calls with tears
streaming down their faces. The results are genuine salvations. These new
converts are then encouraged to fill out a follow-up card. Within days,
trained local counselors visit each one to pray with them and to explain
further this new life in Jesus. The results are often strong new converts.

Besides new church members, there are other valuable benefits from
a gospel crusade. For one thing the gospel is preached in public. The atmosphere is saturated with the message of Jesus Christ crucified and risen from
the dead. The place is plowed and seeded with the Word of God. And no one,
this side of heaven, can fully measure the results. Only God knows the fruit
that may come up in a year, or for that matter, in three years.

I think of David Livingston, the great missionary to Africa, who
had, what seemed to be little fruit during his missionary journey. His
heart is buried in Blantyre, a town in Malawi just a short distance from
where we have held crusades in Chipata, Zambia. Who knows if our
reaping in Chipata may have been in answer to David Livingston's prayer
and the fruit of the gospel he sowed years before. After all, the Scripture
says, "Some reap where others have sown."

On another note, how can one measure the significance of a community wide event where churches and pastors come together in unity to
proclaim Jesus Christ as Lord. The Scriptures say:

> "Behold, how good and how pleasant *it is* for brethren to
> dwell together in unity! *It is* like the precious oil upon the
> head, running down on the beard, the beard of Aaron, run-
> ning down on the edge of his garments. *It is* like the dew of
> Hermon, descending upon the mountains of Zion; for there
> the LORD commanded the blessing—life forevermore"
> (Psalm133:1–3).

As the Churches work, pray and praise together, the community
experiences a unified expression of the body of Christ. The impact of the
gospel is multiplied changing the hearts of men and consequently the
moral climate of the township. There is blessing.

Then, the manifestation of signs, wonders and miracles are a lasting testimony to the love of Jesus. For those who witness them and for those who receive them, there is joy:

> "Then Philip went down to the city of Samaria and preached Christ to them. And the multitudes with one accord heeded the things spoken by Philip, hearing and seeing the miracles, which he did. For unclean spirits, crying with a loud voice, came out of many who were possessed; and many who were paralyzed and lame were healed. And there was great joy in that city" (Acts 8:4–8).

Are gospel crusades effective? The answer is a resounding yes. They are a first step in answer to the call of the Lord to go into all the world and make disciples: "And this gospel of the kingdom will be preached in all the world as a witness to all the nations, and then the end will come" (Matthew 24:14).

Josef's wife Anne Rousek praying for the needy during a crusade.

The worship team dances on the ground.

Lady healed of blind eye and paralyzed arm. She now is able to lift a Bible and see.

Little girl healed of deafness.

A great altar call in Chawama where thousands of souls confessed Jesus Christ as their Lord and Savior (2005).

Left, Pastor Steve Storey prays for man to receive sight in his right eye. Minutes later the man can see perfectly (top).

Endnotes

Chapter 1 Hope for Africa

1. UNICEF, "Africa's Orphaned Generations." New York. November 2003. page. 50. http://www.unicef.org/
2. UNICEF, "Children on the Brink 2002: A Joint Report on Orphan Estimates and Program Strategies." page 25. http://www.unicef.org/publications/index_4378.html

Chapter 2 Wooden Idols

3. Jerry Simpson, "Thresholds." www.thresholds.net/zunil/index.htm.

Chapter 9 The Changing Landscape of World Missions

4. French is the Congo's official language, but it is spoken by relatively few persons. Swahili is widely used in the east, and Lingala is spoken in the west; Tshilaba is also common.
5. See, BBC. http://news.bbc.co.uk/1/shared/spl/hi/pop_ups/quick_guides/04/africa_dr_congo/html/1.stm
6. See, http://www.jesus.org.uk/dawn/1998/dawn9828.html
7. See, http://www.jesus.org.uk/dawn/1998/dawn9828.html
8. See, http://www.jesus.org.uk/dawn/1998/dawn9839.html
9. See, http://www.jesus.org.uk/dawn/1998/dawn9839.html

Chapter 10 Partnering with the Third World Church

10. George Smith, "Life of William Carey: Shoemaker and Missionary." 1909. http://www.biblebelievers.com/carey/

CHAPTER 12 THE CHANGING ROLE OF THE WESTERN CHURCH

11. See, International Mission Board. "People Groups." http://www.imb.org/globalresearch

CHAPTER 13 TIME IS SHORT

12. UNICEF, "Real lives." November 2002. http://www.unicef.org/infobycountry/zambia_1396.html
13. UNAIDS, "Aids Epidemic Update." December 2004. http://www.unaids.org/wad2004
14. UNICEF, "Zambia at a Glance." http://www.unicef.org15. UNAIDS, "Aids Epidemic Update." December 2004. http://www.unaids.org/wad2004
16. UNICEF, "Africa's Orphaned Generation." page. 42. http://www.unicef.org/publications/index_16271.html.
17. UNICEF, "Children on the Brink 2002: A Joint Report on Orphan Estimates and Program Strategies." page. 25. http://www.unicef.org/publications/index_4378.html
18. UINCEF, "Africa's Orphaned Generations." page. 6. http://www.unicef.org/publications

CHAPTER 18 WHY DO I HAVE SO MUCH?

19. Randy Alcorn, "Investing In Eternity." *New Man Magazine*, June 1997. http://www.epm.org/articles/monnewma.html
20. See, the World Food Program. http://www.wfp.org/
21. See, "Global Economic Inequality: Diet Pills for American Pets and Poverty in Some Parts of the World 'When Pets Pop Pills,'" *Newsweek*, October 11, 1999.
22. See, "An AD 2001 reality check: 50 new facts and figures about trends and issues concerning empirical global Christianity today." (from Table 1-1 in "World Christian Trends," William Carey Library, David Barrett & Todd Johnson.)
23. See, "An AD 2001 reality check: 50 new facts and figures about trends and issues concerning empirical global Christianity today."

If this book has been a blessing to you, please pass it on
to a friend and drop us a note at the
following e-mail:

blessed@fhafrica.org

FHI books